Bright Angel Creek Trout Reduction Project

Winter 2010- 2011 Report

Natural Resource Technical Report NPS/GRCA/NRTR—2012/646

Emily C. Omana Smith, Brian D. Healy, William C. Leibfried

National Park Service
Grand Canyon National Park
1824 S. Thompson Street, Suite 200
Flagstaff, Arizona 86001

Daniel P. Whiting
University of Missouri
Department of Fisheries and Wildlife Sciences
302 Anheuser-Busch Natural Resources Building
Columbia, Missouri 65211

December 2012

U.S. Department of the Interior
National Park Service
Natural Resource Stewardship and Science
Fort Collins, Colorado

The National Park Service, Natural Resource Stewardship and Science office in Fort Collins, Colorado publishes a range of reports that address natural resource topics of interest and applicability to a broad audience in the National Park Service and others in natural resource management, including scientists, conservation and environmental constituencies, and the public.

The Natural Resource Technical Report Series is used to disseminate results of scientific studies in the physical, biological, and social sciences for both the advancement of science and the achievement of the National Park Service mission. The series provides contributors with a forum for displaying comprehensive data that are often deleted from journals because of page limitations.

All manuscripts in the series receive the appropriate level of peer review to ensure that the information is scientifically credible, technically accurate, appropriately written for the intended audience, and designed and published in a professional manner. Data in this report were collected and analyzed using methods based on established, peer-reviewed protocols and were analyzed and interpreted within the guidelines of the protocols.

Views, statements, findings, conclusions, recommendations, and data in this report do not necessarily reflect views and policies of the National Park Service, U.S. Department of the Interior. Mention of trade names or commercial products does not constitute endorsement or recommendation for use by the U.S. Government.

This report is available from the Natural Resource Publications Management website (http://www.nature.nps.gov/publications/nrpm/).

Please cite this publication as:

Omana Smith, E. C., B. D. Healy, W. C. Leibfried, and D. W. Whiting. 2012. Bright Angel Creek trout reduction project: Winter 2010-2011 report. Natural Resource Technical Report NPS/GRCA/NRTR—2012/646. National Park Service, Fort Collins, Colorado.

NPS 113/118207, December 2012

Contents

Contents (continued)

Figures

Figures (continued)

Tables

Appendices

Executive Summary

In October, 2010, Grand Canyon National Park reinitiated the Bright Angel Creek Trout Reduction project to enhance native fish populations and contribute towards the fulfillment of humpback chub conservation measures (USFWS 2008) by reducing the populations of non-native brown (*Salmo trutta*) and rainbow trout (*Oncorhynchus mykiss*) (NPS 2006). This project was first initiated in cooperation with the U.S. Fish and Wildlife Service (USFWS) in 2006-2007 (see Sponholtz et al. 2010) following a Feasibility Study conducted in 2002-2003 by SWCA Environmental Consultants (see Leibfried et al. 2005). Another purpose of this project was to partially fulfill the Bureau of Reclamation's commitment under the 2008 Biological Opinion on operation of Glen Canyon Dam (USFWS 2008) to establish population redundancy of humpback chub (*Gila cypha*) in tributary refuges in Grand Canyon National Park. This report covers weir and electrofishing activities conducted in Bright Angel Creek from October 2010-September 2011.

A weir was operated in lower Bright Angel Creek from October 26, 2010 through February 4, 2011. In total, 105 brown trout and 107 rainbow trout were removed. Two electrofishing trips (October 26-30, 2010 and January 24- February 5, 2011) were conducted in the creek to assess the populations of native and non-native fishes and to remove trout. A total of 489 brown trout and 347 rainbow trout were removed from 2100 meters of stream during two electrofishing trips (October 26-30, 2010 and January 24 – February 5, 2011). Trophic studies were conducted in November 2010 and January, June, and September 2011 to examine the diets of and competitive interactions between native and non-native fishes in the creek, including piscivory. In accordance with the Grand Canyon National Park policy of beneficial use, developed in consultation with Traditionally Associated Indian Tribes, 87% of the trout removed from the creek were consumed by humans.

While the weir was effective at intercepting adult trout, expanding the time frame of weir operations would encompass more of the spawning periods of brown and rainbow trout. After 2 electrofishing trips, trout were found to have recolonized the removal stretches from locations higher upstream in the creek. In order to maintain low levels of non-native trout, removal efforts should also be expanded to cover larger portions of the creek and prevent recolonization.

Acknowledgments

The project was funded through an interagency agreement with the U. S Bureau of Reclamation and the National Park Service. Trophic and diet studies were funded with a Cooperative Ecosystems Studies Unit cooperative agreement with the University of Missouri and USGS Cooperative Fish and Wildlife Research Unit. Volunteer support was provided in part by Grand Canyon Trust. The planning and implementation of this project benefitted from input from and cooperation with many Divisions within Grand Canyon National Park. The authors would like to specifically thank the Phantom Ranch Rangers and Interpretation staff, VIP Sjors, NPS mule packers and mules, NPS helibase crew, Phantom Ranch Maintenance and Treatment Plant personnel, Phantom Ranch Trail Crew bunkhouse, as well as M. Trammell, D. Speas, M. Crawford, J. Spurgeon, P. Sponholtz, U.S. Fish and Wildlife Service, volunteers, M. Wunner, G. Utech, P. Wallace-Geiger, A. Mathis, M. Tighe, J. Reimer, L. Joe, L. Whetton, M. Hahn, J. Balsom, and J. Rodgers. The following scientists communicated relevant information with B. Healy that was used in this report: J. Korman, W. Persons, and D. Topping. Technical review was provided by J. Wullschleger, M. Trammell, and M. Crawford, who all provided valuable comments and edits.

Introduction

Background

In October, 2010, Grand Canyon National Park reinitiated the Bright Angel Creek Trout Reduction project to enhance native fish populations and contribute towards the fulfillment of humpback chub conservation measures (USFWS 2008) by reducing the populations of non-native brown (*Salmo trutta*) and rainbow trout (*Oncorhynchus mykiss*) (NPS 2006). This report summarizes 2010-2011 Bright Angel Creek efforts to remove non-native fish species from Bright Angel Creek using a weir and electrofishing, and to continue to assess the effects of non-native fishes on native species via competition for food or predation. Another purpose of this project is to partially fulfill the Bureau of Reclamation's commitment under the 2008 Biological Opinion on operation of Glen Canyon Dam (USFWS 2008) to establish population redundancy of humpback chub in tributary refuges in Grand Canyon National Park:

> In coordination with other Department of the Interior (DOI) AMP [Adaptive Management Program] participants and through the AMP, Reclamation will assist NPS [National Park Service] and the AMP in funding and implementation of translocation of humpback chub into tributaries of the Colorado River in Marble and Grand canyons. Nonnative control in these tributaries will be an essential precursor to translocation, so Reclamation will help fund control of both cold and warm-water nonnative fish in tributaries, as well as efforts to translocate humpback chub into these tributaries. Havasu, Shinumo, and Bright Angel creeks will initially be targeted for translocation, although other tributaries may be considered. Reclamation will work with FWS [U.S. Fish and Wildlife Service], NPS and other cooperators to develop translocation plans for each of these streams, utilizing existing information available such as Grand Canyon Wildlands Council and SWCA (2006) and Valdez et al. (2000). These plans will consider and utilize genetic assessments (Douglas and Douglas 2007, DNFHTC 2010), identify legal requirements and jurisdictional issues, methods, and assess needs for nonnative control, monitoring and other logistics, as well as an implementation schedule, funding sources, and permitting. Reclamation and the AMP will also fund and implement translocation of up to 500 young humpback chub from the lower Little Colorado River to above Chute Falls in 2008 if FWS determines that a translocation is warranted. Reclamation and the AMP will continue to monitor humpback chub in the reach of the Little Colorado River above Chute Falls for the 5-year period of the proposed action, and will undertake additional translocations above Chute Falls as deemed necessary by FWS.

Tributary translocations may also provide grow-out habitats for young humpback chub that can subsequently disperse to the mainstream and augment the existing aggregations of humpback chub (Valdez and Ryel 1995). The restoration of native fish, through translocation and the control of non-native fish, is consistent with NPS Management Policies (2006) and the Grand Canyon National Park General Management Plan (1995). These activities may also potentially result in range expansion of humpback chub and the establishment of a second spawning aggregation in Grand Canyon National Park.

Translocation of wild, young-of-year humpback chub is planned from the Little Colorado River to Shinumo, Havasu, and Bright Angel Creeks over a period of five years (2009-2014). Translocations into Shinumo and Havasu Creeks are currently underway (GCWC 2010, Healy et al. 2011a, Healy et al. 2011b, Sponholtz et al. 2011). The Bright Angel Creek Trout Reduction project is an important pre-cursor to translocations of humpback chub into Bright Angel Creek, which supports a large population of non-native trout (Carothers and Minckley 1981, Otis 1994, Leibfried et al. 2005, Sponholtz et al. 2010). Ideally, non-native fish would be completely removed from a tributary prior to translocation of humpback chub to minimize the need for long-term management and non-native control activities.

In the Colorado River in Grand Canyon, non-native rainbow trout (*Oncorhynchus mykiss*) and brown trout (*Salmo trutta)* compete with and selectively prey upon humpback chub (*Gila cypha*) and other native fishes (Valdez and Ryel 1995, Gloss and Coggins 2005, Yard et al. 2011, Coggins et al. 2011). Bright Angel Creek and areas nearby in the Colorado River historically supported thriving populations of native fish, including endangered humpback chub. As recently as the 1970s, brown trout, a trout species native to Europe and Asia, were rare in Bright Angel Creek (Minckley 1978, Otis 1994). Since the 1990s however, they have become a large component of the fish community in the creek, and a corresponding decline in native fish such as speckled dace (*Rhinichthys osculus*) has been observed (Otis 1994). Bright Angel Creek is now an important spawning site for brown trout, and a large aggregation of brown trout is found in the Colorado River near the confluence with Bright Angel Creek (Speas 2002, Makinster et al. 2010).

Non-native fish removals have been implemented sporadically in Grand Canyon both in the mainstem Colorado River (see Coggins et al. 2011) and in tributaries such as Shinumo and Bright Angel creeks (see GCWC 2010, Sponholtz et al. 2010, Healy et al. 2011a, and Healy et al. 2011b). It can be difficult to evaluate the effectiveness of such efforts due to the influence of confounding factors such as temperature changes (see Coggins et al. 2011) and to logistical challenges such as gear and sampling limitations (see GCWC 2010, Healy et al. 2011a).

History
During the winter of 2002-2003, NPS contracted SWCA Environmental Consultants to conduct a feasibility study testing the effectiveness of a weir in Bright Angel Creek. The feasibility study lasted for 64 days from November 18, 2002- January 21, 2003, and 423 brown trout were removed from the creek (Leibfried et al. 2005).

In 2006, NPS completed an Environmental Assessment/ Assessment of Effect (EA) on the Bright Angel Creek Trout Reduction Project and issued a Finding of No Significant Impact (FONSI; NPS 2006). The selected alternative stated:

> Under Alternative B, all non-native fish, primarily brown trout and rainbow trout, would be mechanically removed from Bright Angel Creek using 1) a weir to capture them as they move upstream into the creek to spawn, and 2) electrofishing and dip netting (depletion sampling) in conjunction with weir use as part of fish community response monitoring to determine the effects of the project on the fish community in the creek.

A weir was installed and operated by the U.S. Fish and Wildlife Service (FWS) on two occasions in 2006-2007. During the first installation of 71 days from November 11, 2006- January 23, 2007, 54 brown trout were removed from Bright Angel Creek (Sponholtz et al. 2010). The weir was installed a second time for 36 days from April 6- May 11, 2007; no trout were captured during this time period (Sponholtz et al. 2010). Fish response was also monitored in Bright Angel Creek during a spring and a fall backpack electrofishing trip; 158 and 311 brown trout were removed during those efforts (Sponholtz et al. 2010).

Objectives

The dual purposes of the project are described in the FONSI (NPS 2006) for the Bright Angel Creek Trout Reduction project, including the removal of non-native fish, primarily trout, to benefit endangered humpback chub and other native fish species in the mainstem Colorado River, and to restore and enhance, to the extent possible, the native fish community that once flourished in Bright Angel Creek. In addition, project activities were meant to partially fulfill the intent of the conservation measures of the 2008 Biological Opinion for the operations of Glen Canyon Dam. Specific objectives were to:

1. Install and operate the weir to capture migratory trout moving into Bright Angel Creek to spawn from the Colorado River.
2. Remove non-native fishes from Bright Angel Creek upstream of the weir using backpack electrofishing gear.
3. Monitor the native and non-native fish community abundance (population size) and composition in Bright Angel Creek using multiple-pass electrofishing.
4. Collect samples to assess trophic position of native and non-native fish in Bright Angel Creek.
5. Interpret project objectives and methods to Phantom Ranch staff and park visitors.

Methods

Study Area

Bright Angel Creek is a perennial tributary of the Colorado River, entering the river from the Kaibab Plateau and North Rim at approximately river mile 88 (Figure 1). This second order stream flows south for approximately 19 kilometers from Angel Springs, fed by several other springs along the way (Usher et al. 1984). Bright Angel Creek has a mean annual discharge of 35 cubic feet per second (NPS 2006) and a gradient of 55 meters per kilometer (Huntoon 1970, Usher et al. 1984). Water temperatures in Bright Angel Creek vary from 2.1°C to 30.2°C (Voichick and Wright 2007). There are no barriers to fish movement between the Colorado River and Bright Angel Creek, although there are barrier falls further upstream in the creek.

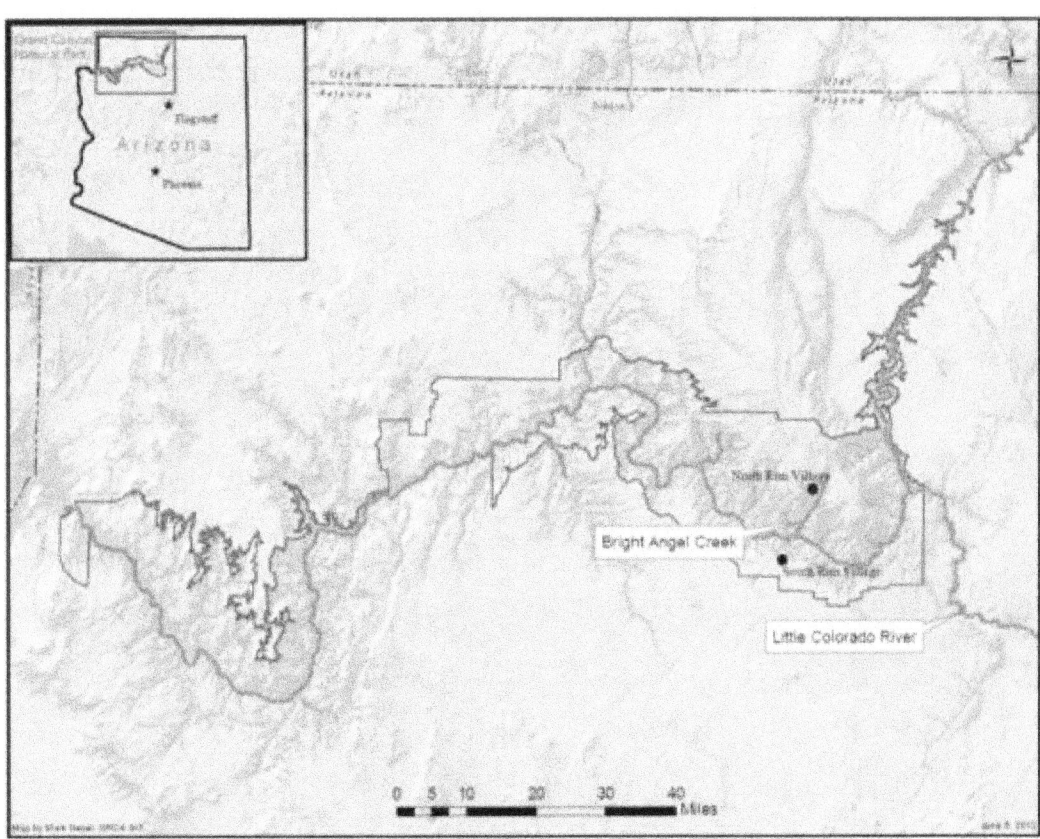

Figure1. Bright Angel Creek is located in Grand Canyon National Park, Arizona.

Weir

Weir and electrofishing activities were performed in Bright Angel Creek in Grand Canyon National Park, Arizona (Figure 1). The weir used in Bright Angel Creek (Figure 2) was constructed to capture spawning trout by SWCA Environmental Consultants in 2002 according to a design by the Wyoming Game and Fish Department (Leibfried et al. 2005). It consisted of four 10 foot long panels separated by a 3 foot by 4 foot trap with an opening on the downstream end (Figure 2, Figure 3a). Rebar and fencing T-posts were anchored in the creek substrate, serving to hold the panels together and attach them to the trap. The panels were lined with aluminum rods that created a barrier to fish movement, considered impassable for fish greater

5

than 200 millimeters in total length (TL). The trap was lined with small gauge mesh and covered with a hinged lid allowing for fish removal; the lid was kept locked. A review of previous weir operations (Leibfried et al. 2005; FWS/NPS data) revealed that trout greater than approximately 200 mm total length are captured in the weir. It is likely that fish smaller than this size could pass through the mesh covering the trap or through the aluminum rods in the side panels (13 mm spacing); however, no testing was completed to assess size-related bias in the gear.

The weir was installed under the bridge crossing Bright Angel Creek closest to the Colorado River (Figure 2) on October 26, 2010 and operated continuously until December 19, 2010, when it was damaged by a flood in the creek. Initially, with the onset of flooding, some of the aluminum rods were removed to reduce pressure on the weir components, but on December 21 the weir was damaged (Figure 3b) and subsequently removed. It was replaced in the creek in the same location on December 27, 2010, and operated continuously until February 4, 2010.

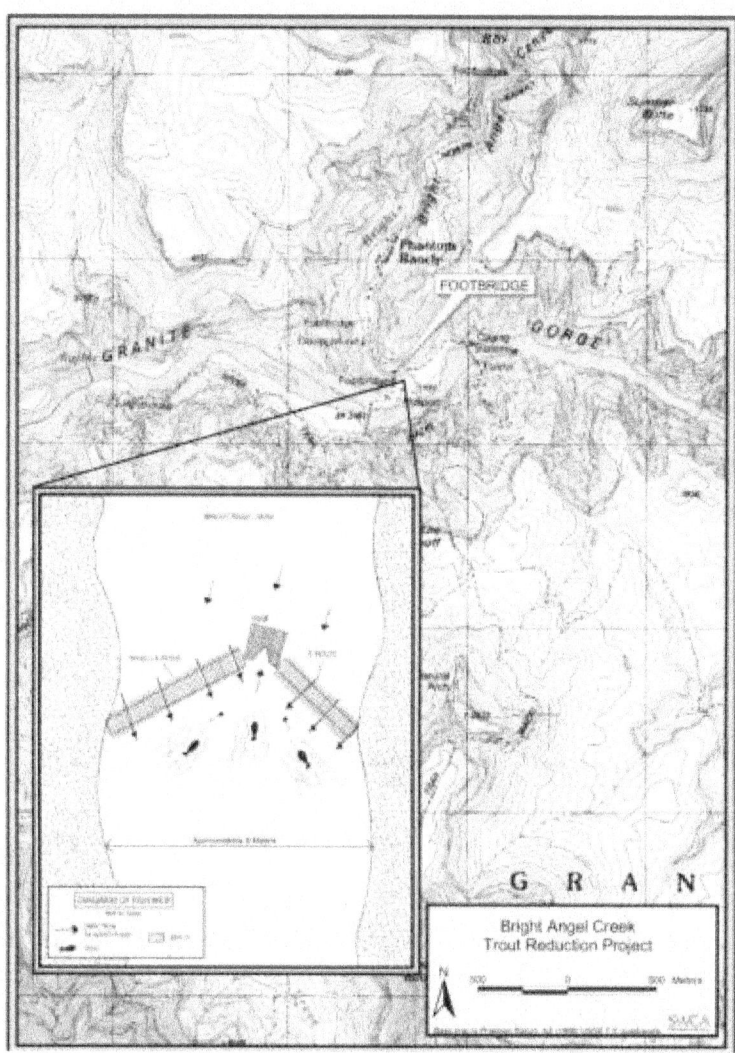

Figure 2. Location of weir in Bright Angel Creek, Grand Canyon National Pak. Inset: schematic drawing of weir. Map and diagram by SWCA Environmental Consultants.

A biologist was on site throughout the entirety of the weir operation (Appendix A). The weir was checked twice each day: once in the morning and once in the evening. The time and date of each check were recorded as well as the water temperature and the operator's name. All captured fish were removed from the trap and the following data were collected: species; total length (mm); fork length (mm); weight (grams); sex, sexual condition, and sexual characteristics; recapture (yes or no), including the presence of any fin clips, VIE tags, PIT tags, or Floy tags and their descriptions; stomach contents of non-native species, and disposition of specimens. If captured, native fish were to be released above the weir, and non-natives were humanely euthanized and saved for human consumption (see *Beneficial Use* below). In captured female trout, the weight of the entire egg mass (grams) and the weight of 100 eggs were recorded to the nearest 0.1 gram, allowing for the gravimetric estimation of the total fecundity of the individual.

Figure 3a. The weir installed in Bright Angel Creek in 2010-11 during normal operations (NPS photograph by Maddie Tighe).

Figure 3b. Flooding in Bright Angel Creek disabled the weir, which was non-functional (as above) or removed from December 19-26, 2010 while flow subsided (photograph by Dan Whiting).

Electrofishing

Three-pass electrofishing was used during two trips to generate population estimates for native and non-native fish in Bright Angel Creek and to remove trout. Three-pass depletion electrofishing was conducted in 6 approximately 100-meter block-netted stations between the weir and just upstream of the Phantom Ranch Ranger Station from October 27- 29, 2010 (602 meters total). Additional days of electrofishing had been planned in October; however these were not possible as weather conditions delayed helicopter transport of gear to Phantom Ranch. During a second trip from January 25- February 3, 2011, three-pass depletion electrofishing was conducted in 15 of 16 approximately 100-meter block-netted stations (1650 meters total). Only 2 passes were conducted in one of these stations due to time constraints. Also in January, an additional single pass was conducted for 450 meters upstream of the depletion stations, ending at the first trail bridge above Phantom Ranch.

In general, Smith-Root LR-20B (400 watt) backpack electrofishing units were set at 350 volts (V) and 30% duty cycle, with an output frequency of 35 hertz (Hz). In October, voltage was initially set at 250 V, and then responses of fish were monitored, and then increased to 350 V when fish appeared to be minimally affected by the current. In January, voltage was initially set at 350 V, the setting used in previous trips; this was quickly reduced to 300 V when injuries to trout were observed during the first pass. It is unclear however, if the observed injuries were related to electrofishing, as voltage was later increased again to 350 V within large pools and faster habitats upstream with no apparent ill-effects to fish collected. After capture, fish were monitored for impacts from the gear while in buckets. Injuries were not apparent, and fish were observed to recover quickly after capture, so settings remained unchanged throughout the remainder of the survey.

Two tandem electrofishing units were used to cover the entire stream width, followed closely by survey teams of 4 netters and 1-2 bucket tenders (7-8 total personnel). For one day during the October sampling event (October 28), only 6 total personnel completed the survey, requiring a team member to operate the electrofishing unit and net at the same time. All captured fish > 150 mm were scanned for a PIT (passive integrated transponder) tag, weighed (in grams), measured (total length, TL; and fork length, FL, in mm), and native fish were released below the downstream block net following the PIT-tagging of any untagged fish. Speckled dace (*Rhinichthys osculus*) and bluehead sucker (*Catostomus discobolus*) <150 mm were measured, weighed, and returned to the stream below sampling reaches between passes. All non-native fish were humanely euthanized and prepared for human consumption (see ***Beneficial Use*** below).

Depletion Sampling Analysis

Fish population estimates generated using data collected through depletion sampling have been found to be biased low for trout due to size-selectivity of the gear and behavioral responses to electrofishing (Peterson et al. 2004, summarized in Saunders et al. 2011). In addition, differences in habitat complexity across sites may influence capture probability. To account for size- and behavior-related biases, population estimates and 95% confidence intervals for trout were calculated with Program MARK using analytical methods described in Saunders et al. (2011). An advantage of the conditional likelihood methods in Program MARK (White and Burnham 1999) is that both site-specific and individual heterogeneity can be accounted for by including individual covariates such as fish length in the analysis (Huggins closed-capture data type, White

2008). Data can also be pooled from multiple sites to derive capture probability parameters for abundance estimation.

Various *a priori* models were analyzed using Program MARK including combinations of factors that may influence fish capture probability, including fish total length (trout only), season of sampling (October and January), sampling pass (1st pass vs. 2nd and 3rd passes), and species. The model that best explained the variation in the data (i.e., most parsimonious) was selected using the Akaike Information Criterion as described in Cooch and White (2011).

An estimate of the overall brown and rainbow trout and speckled dace abundance from all stations for each sampling trip was calculated, incorporating data collected from 602 meters (6 depletion stations) in October and 1538 meters (15 depletion stations) in January. Data from site 11 in January were excluded from analysis because only two sampling passes were conducted. Abundance estimates and confidence intervals were then standardized to an estimate of the average number (density) of fish per 100 meters.

The removal efficiency (i.e., percent of trout removed) for 3-pass depletion was calculated with average capture probabilities (q) estimated using Program MARK for the most parsimonious abundance estimation model as described above, and the following equation:

$$percent\ of\ trout\ removed = [1 - (1-q)^3] \times 100.$$

Other Removal Methods
Angling was used to remove rainbow and brown trout from Bright Angel Creek, both in the electrofishing areas above the weir, as well as below the weir. Both spinning and fly fishing techniques were used. Whenever captured, both trout species were euthanized and prepared for human consumption. Other angling in the study area also occurred by private citizens during weir and electrofishing operations.

Beneficial Use
As determined through consultation with Traditionally Associated Tribes, trout removed from Bright Angel Creek were consumed by humans, within the limits of safety. Trout were kept alive as long as possible in live wells until they could be processed for consumption. Trout that died and began to decompose were discarded away from the creek and trails, or where they could be spotted and consumed by ravens and other wildlife. Once processed, trout were placed in a portable smoker for approximately 2 – 2 ½ hours or pan fried, and eaten. Smoked trout not immediately consumed were placed in a freezer for later consumption.

Trophic and Diet Sampling
Stable isotopes and stomach contents of brown and rainbow trout were analyzed to assess diet overlap and trophic position of native and non-native fishes in Bright Angel Creek. Samples from fishes, invertebrates, and basal resources were collected during electrofishing trips in October 2010 and January 2011, as well as in June and September 2011. For stable isotope analyses, pelvic fin clips from a minimum of 5 individuals of each species (speckled dace, bluehead sucker, brown trout, and rainbow trout) were collected, air dried, and preserved in salt. Stomachs of brown and rainbow trout were collected from at least one fish within the following

size-classes: 50-100, 101-200, 201-300, >300 (mm TL) and preserved in 10% formalin. Aquatic invertebrates were sampled in riffles and pools using a Hess sampler. Sweep nets were used to collect terrestrial invertebrates along riparian and upland vegetation zones. Dominant aquatic and terrestrial invertebrates (Ephemeroptera, Trichoptera, Megaloptera, Diptera, and Orthoptera) were identified and sorted in the field and aquatic taxa were stored in freshwater overnight to allow for gut evacuation. Basal resources, including detritus from debris piles, filamentous algae, periphyton, and dominant bank vegetation (willow and cottonwood) were collected during each sampling period and placed into sealed plastic bags. Invertebrate samples were air dried and stored in salt for preservation, and basal resource samples were frozen until laboratory processing.

In the laboratory, pelvic fin clips, invertebrates, and basal resource samples were rinsed with Barnstead purified water (Barnstead Co., Boston, MA), dried for 48 hours at 55°C, and homogenized using a mortar and pestle. Powdered samples were analyzed by the University of Missouri biogeochemistry lab using a Finnigan Delta-Plus gas source mass spectrometer to measure $\delta^{13}C$ and $\delta^{15}N$ signatures. Stable isotope bi-plots were constructed comparing the amount of $\delta^{13}C$ and $\delta^{15}N$ among fish species, fish size classes, invertebrates, and organic matter. Stomachs of brown and rainbow trout were dissected under a microscope where all contents were examined and classified as fish, aquatic invertebrates, terrestrial invertebrates, or organic matter. Sorted contents were then dried for 48 hours at 55°C and weighed to the nearest 0.001 gram to estimate dry mass of each category.

Public Outreach
NPS interpretation personnel worked with NPS fisheries biologists to create a poster for display at Phantom Ranch near the location of the weir (Appendix B). This poster described the project and the weir, and offered contact information for interested parties.

Park managers considered the project to be an important outreach opportunity for discussing the ecological significance of Grand Canyon's native fish with park visitors. During weir operations and electrofishing trips, biologists discussed the project with Phantom Ranch visitors as well as NPS and Xanterra employees; interactions were recorded in a log book. Wherever possible, information recorded included the approximate number of people in each group, relative length of contact, opinion of the project (if expressed), home location, purpose of trip (work, pleasure, angling, etc.), and any other pertinent information related to the contact.

Results

A total of 3,447 fish were captured in Bright Angel Creek during 2010-11 weir and electrofishing efforts (Table 1). Speckled dace were the most common species collected (67.4%, 2,323), followed by brown trout (17.5%, 603), rainbow trout (13.9%, 480), and bluehead sucker (1.2%, 41) (Table 1). No other fish species were collected during electrofishing or weir efforts.

Table 1. Fish captures by method in Bright Angel Creek, October 26, 2010 – February 4, 2011.

	Weir	Electrofishing		Angling	Totals	
	Oct. 26, 2010-Feb. 4, 2011*	Oct. 26-30, 2010	Jan. 25-Feb. 3, 2011	various	Fish Captures	Relative Abundance (%)
Bluehead sucker						
Catostomus discobolus	0	4	37	0	41	1.2
Speckled dace						
Rhinicthys osculus	0	992	1331	0	2323	67.4
Brown trout						
Salmo trutta	105	125	364	9	603	17.5
Rainbow trout						
Oncorhynchus mykiss	107	104	243	26	480	13.9
Total	212	1225	1975	35	3447	100

*Weir was non-functional from December 19-26, 2010 due to high creek flows.

Weir Captures

The weir was operated from October 26, 2010 until February 4, 2011 with the exception of 8 days from December 19 and 26, 2010 during flooding in Bright Angel Creek (Figure 3b). The weir was operational for 93 total days. A total of 212 adult fish were captured in the weir (Table 1), consisting of 105 brown trout and 107 rainbow trout. No other species or juvenile fish were caught in the weir. Daily weir catches ranged from 0-17 fish per day, with most fish captured in the morning. Average catch-per-unit-effort (CPUE) for the weir operations was 2.3 fish/ day (1.1 and 1.2 brown and rainbow trout per day, respectively). Brown trout dominated catches in November and dropped in number in January (Figure 4a). Rainbow trout were caught sporadically in November; catches increased in December. The majority of fish caught in the weir in January were rainbow trout (Figure 4b). Of the 105 total brown trout captured, 47% (49/105) were collected during a total of five days (November 3: 11 BNT, December 4-6: 30 BNT, December 17: 8 BNT; Figure 4a). Eighty-four percent (88/105) of all brown trout captures occurred between November 3 and December 17 (Figure 4a). Of the 107 rainbow trout captured with the weir, a 4 day time period (December 4-7) resulted in 22% (23/107) of the total collected (Figure 4b).

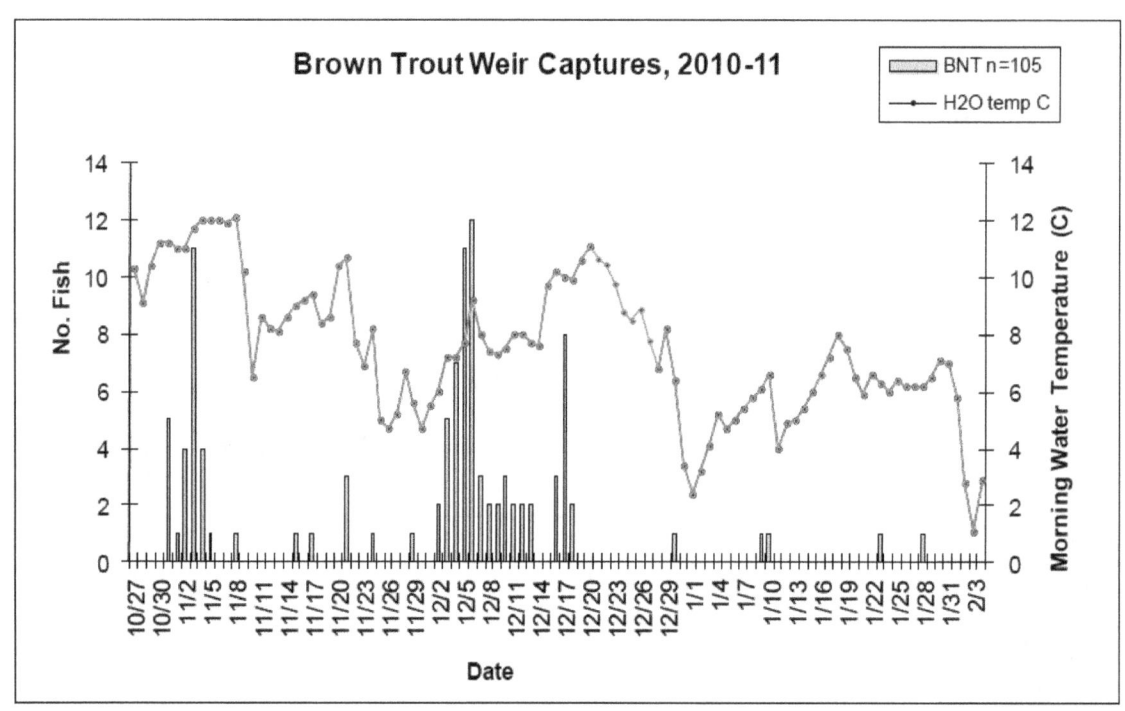

Figure 4a. Weir captures by date and morning water temperature in Bright Angel Creek for brown trout. The weir was disabled from December 19-26 due to flooding.

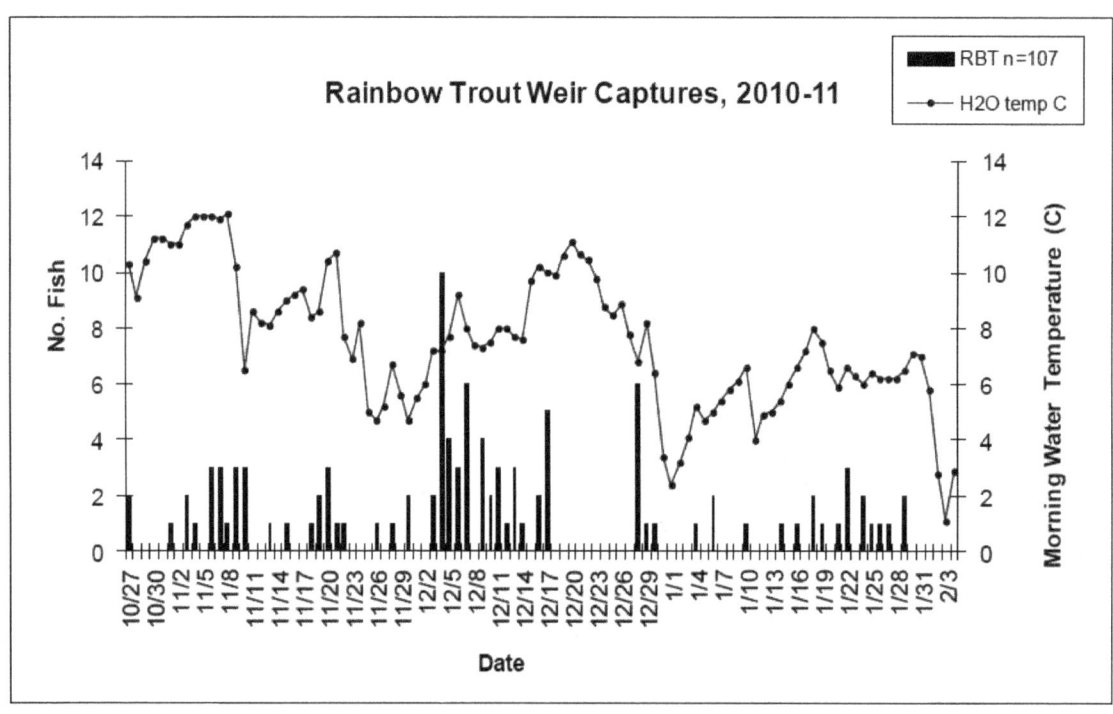

Figure 4b. Weir captures by date and morning water temperature in Bright Angel Creek for rainbow trout. The weir was disabled from December 19-26 due to flooding.

12

Morning water temperature in Bright Angel Creek ranged from 1.1°C. to 12.1°C (Figure 4). Mean water temperature for brown trout captures was 9.2°C (range= 5.6-12.1°C; Figure 5a) and did not differ for day versus night captures (*t*-test, *p* = 0.73; Figure 5a). The same pattern was observed for rainbow trout captures- mean water temperature was 8.2°C (95% CI= 4.7-12.1°C) and capture temperature did not differ significantly between day and night (*t*-test, *p* = 0.15; Figure 5a). Brown and rainbow trout captures only occurred when morning water temperatures were not significantly different from evening temperatures (*t*-test, BNT: *p* = 0.073, RBT: *p* = 0.15; Figure 5a). During times when no fish were captured in the weir, the temperatures were significantly different between day and night samples (*t*-test, *p* << 0.001; Figure 5a). Capture frequency was significantly different between day and night catches for both brown trout (χ2 test, *p* << 0.0001; Figure 5b) and rainbow trout (χ2 test, *p* << 0.0001; Figure 5b).

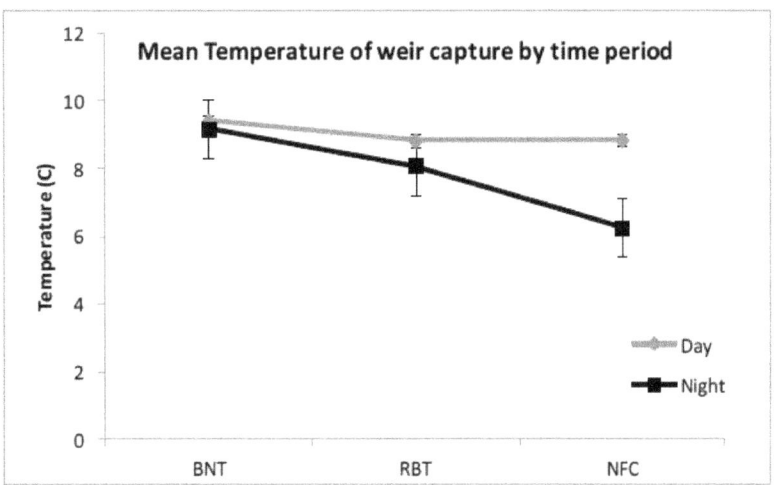

Figure 5a. Mean water temperature, in degrees Celsius, of day and night weir catches of brown trout (*p* = 0.073) and rainbow trout (*p* = 0.15) as well as times in which no fish were caught (NFC, *p* << 0.0001) in Bright Angel Creek.

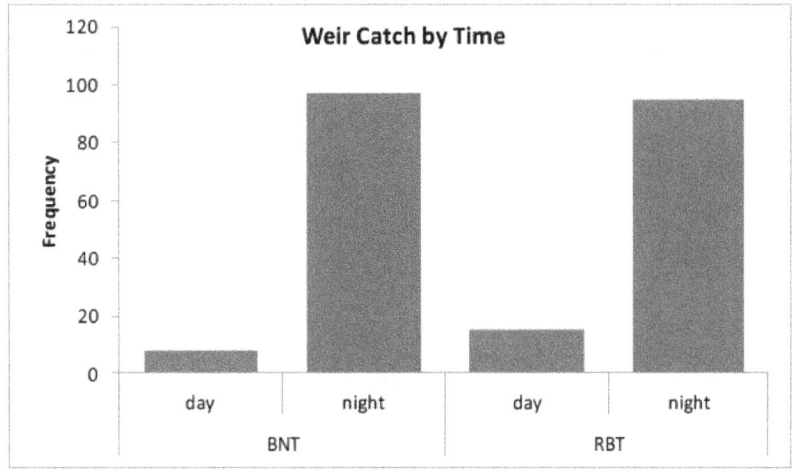

Figure 5b. Capture frequency by sampling period for brown trout (*p* << 0.0001) and rainbow trout (*p* << 0.0001) captures in Bright Angel Creek.

Brown trout captures

The mean total length of brown trout captured using the weir was 383 mm (95% CI= 351-378 mm; range = 136-634 mm; Figure 6). Forty-five brown trout were weighed; the mean weight was 542 grams (95% CI= 471-612) and the range of weights was 105-1430 grams. Seventy-three brown trout were ripe (i.e. gametes were extrudable with light pressure) (69.5%), 31 were not ripe (29.5%) and 1 was undetermined (1%); sex ratio (# males: # females) was significantly female-skewed at 38:66 (χ2 test, p = 0.006). In brown trout, fecundity (total number of eggs) was strongly correlated with both body weight (n = 45; logistic regression, R^2 = 0.94: Figure 7a) and with total body length (logistic regression, R^2 = 0.86; Figure 7b).

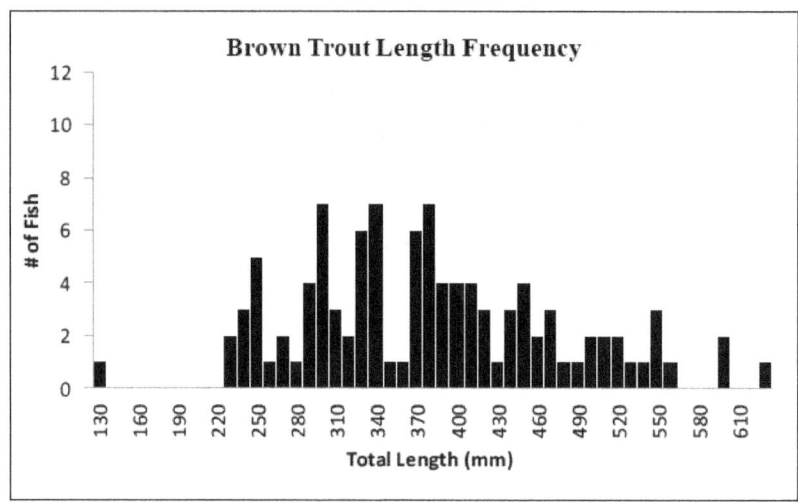

Figure 6. Length frequency histograms for Bright Angel Creek weir-captured brown trout.

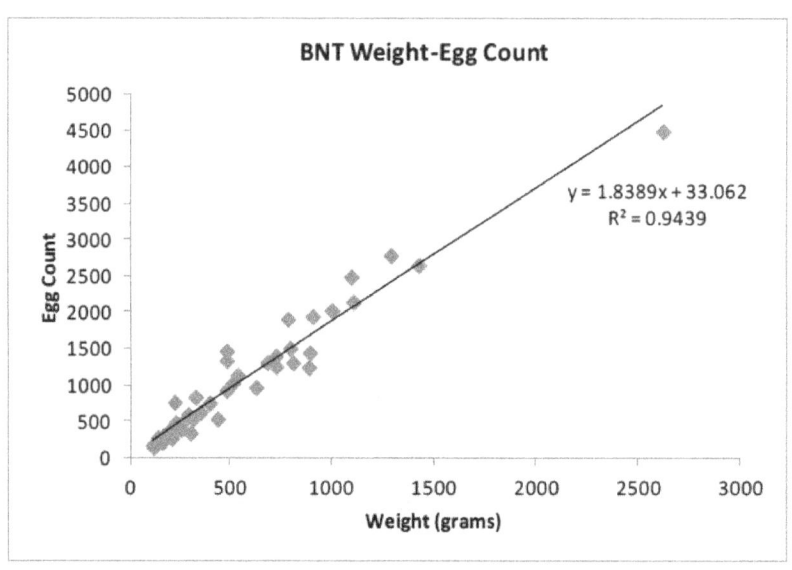

Figure 7a. Correlation of fecundity and weight in brown trout collected using the weir in Bright Angel Creek.

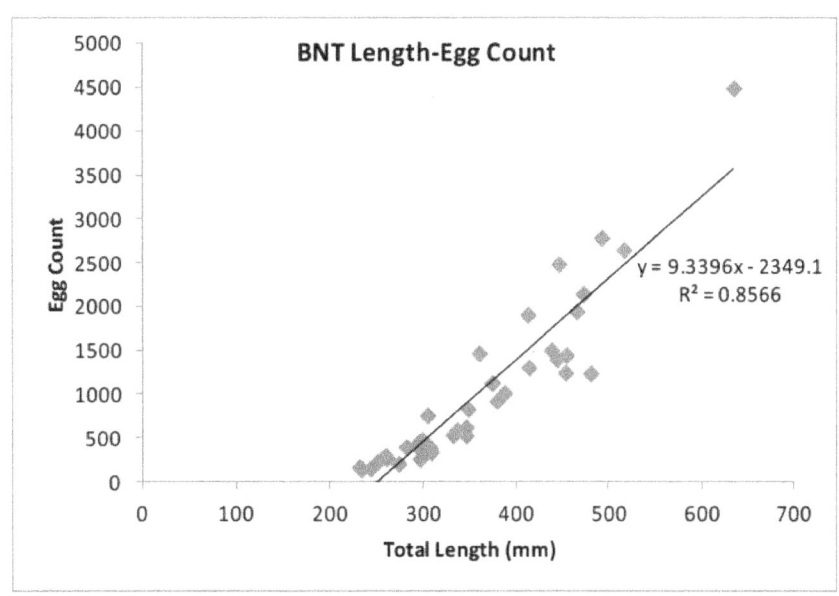

Figure 7b. Correlation of fecundity and total length in brown trout collected using the weir in Bright Angel Creek.

Based on stomach contents analysis, 77% (85/110) of brown trout intercepted by the weir had empty stomachs (Figure 8). The remaining 23% contained invertebrates (14 occurrences), algae/ detritus (4 occurrences), other (3 occurrences), fish/ fish parts (2 occurrences), and fish eggs (2 occurrences) (Figure 8).

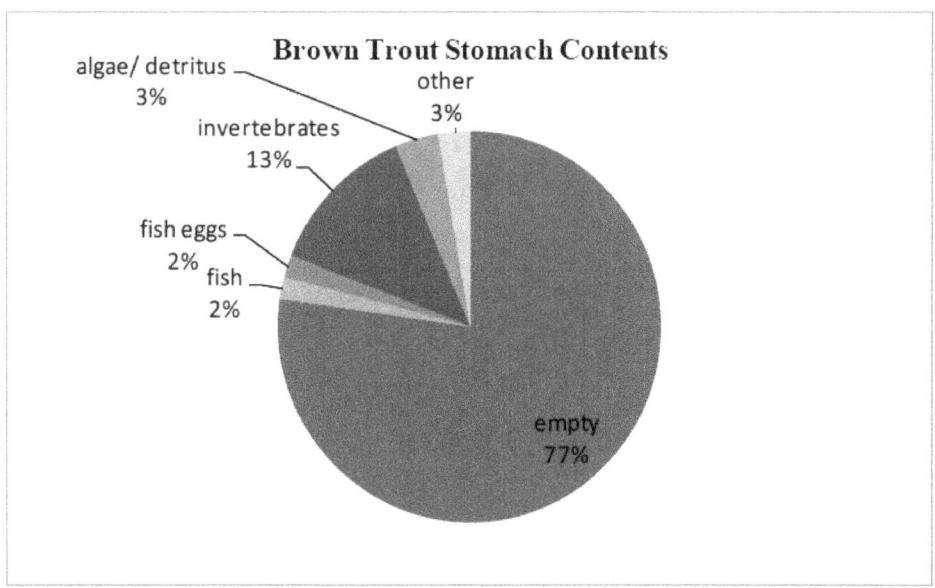

Figure 8. Stomach contents of brown trout collected in Bright Angel Creek using the weir.

Rainbow trout captures

Rainbow trout captured in the weir had a mean total length of 358 mm (95% CI= 325-370 mm) and ranged in size from 227-596 mm (Figure 9). Mean rainbow trout weight was 437 grams (95% CI= 396-478) and the range was 130-1300 grams, measured from 31 fish. Of rainbow trout captured in the weir, 79 were ripe (73.8%), 25 were not ripe (23.4%), and 3 were undetermined (2.8%). The sex ratio of rainbow trout was statistically even at 61:44 ($\chi2$ test, $p = 0.10$). Rainbow trout body weight (n = 31, logistic regression, R^2= 0.67; Figure 10a) and length (logistic regression, R^2= 0.63; Figure 10b) were poorer predictors of fecundity than for brown trout.

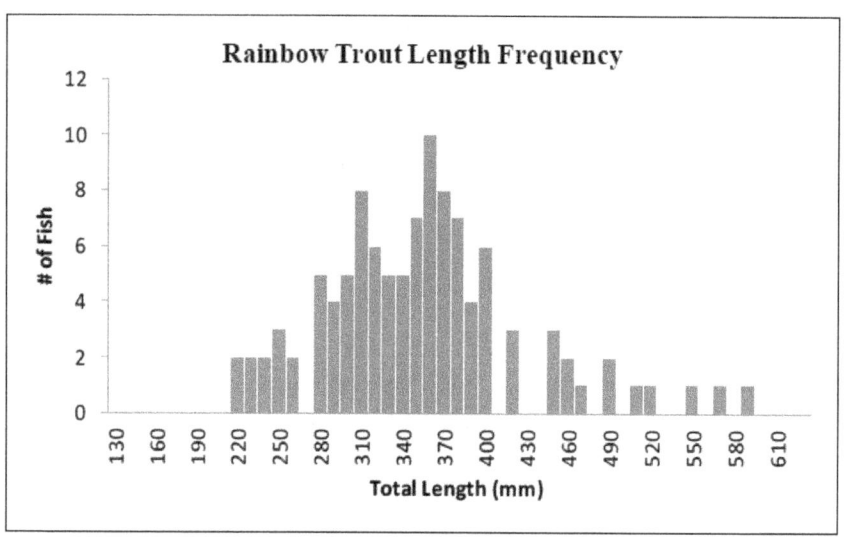

Figure 9. Length frequency histograms for Bright Angel Creek weir-captured rainbow trout.

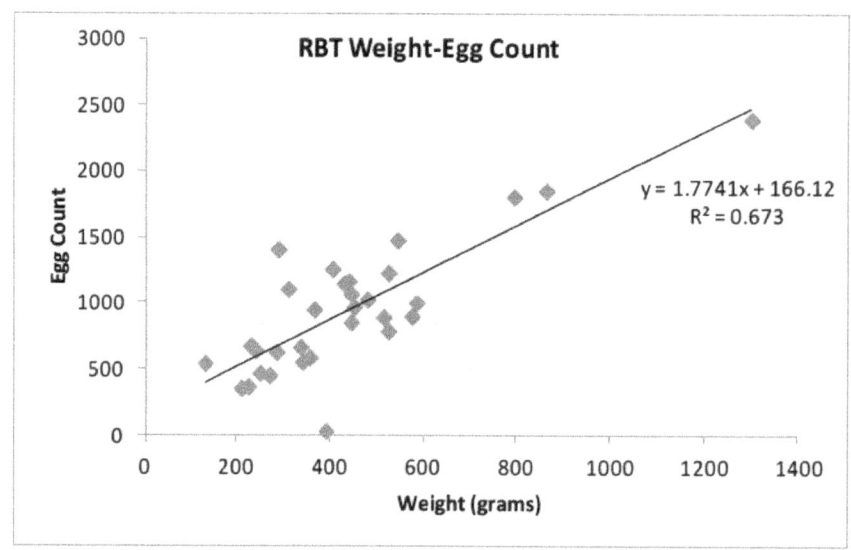

Figure 10a. Correlation of fecundity and weight in rainbow trout collected using the weir in Bright Angel Creek.

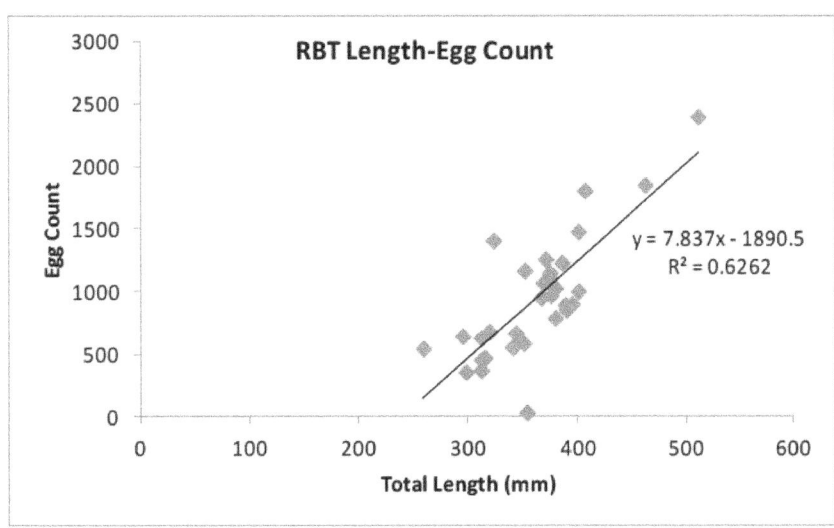

Figure 10b. Correlation of fecundity and total length in rainbow trout collected using the weir in Bright Angel Creek.

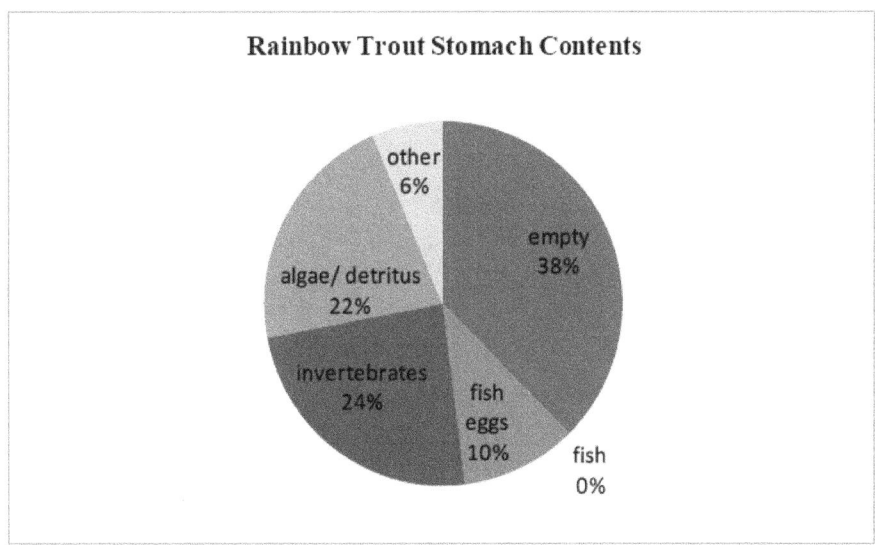

Figure 11. Stomach contents of rainbow trout collected in Bright Angel Creek using the weir.

Thirty-eight percent (47/125) of rainbow trout stomachs were empty (Figure 11). The remaining 62% contained invertebrates (30 occurrences), algae/ detritus (27 occurrences), fish eggs (13 occurrences), and other uncategorized objects (8 occurrences, Figure 11).

Thirteen previously tagged brown and rainbow trout were recaptured during weir operations (Table 2). The USGS - Grand Canyon Monitoring and Research Center (GCMRC) maintains the centralized database of fish captures in Grand Canyon and its tributaries. However, only 5 brown trout and 2 rainbow trout of the 13 total tagged trout captured in the weir were located in the

GCMRC centralized fish database; the remaining 6 were unaccounted for as of December 2011. Of the records that were located, 4 brown trout were initially tagged in the mainstem Colorado River from 2005-2010 within 10 miles of the Bright Angel Creek confluence (river mile 88.3). One rainbow trout was initially tagged in 2009 in the mainstem Colorado River just upstream of the Little Colorado River (River Mile 60.2), important habitat and spawning grounds for the largest remaining aggregation of endangered humpback chub. A second rainbow trout, tagged in 2010, was near another humpback chub aggregation at river mile 30.5. One bluehead sucker was also recaptured in February 2011 that was originally tagged during USFWS electrofishing efforts in Bright Angel Creek in May 2007 (Table 2).

Table 2. Bright Angel Creek weir and electrofishing recaptures. Gray rows indicate records not located in the centralized GCMRC fish database.

Species	Total Length (mm)	Weight (g)	Sex	PIT or FLOY Tag number	Date Tagged	Date of Weir Capture	Days at Large	Location Tagged (RM)	Initial Length/ Weight
Brown Trout	390	521	Female	3D9.1C2D17D301	4/1/2009	11/4/2010	582	86.4	367
Brown Trout	330	305	Male	3D9.1C2D2132F3	4/2/2009	11/5/2010	582	88.5	263
Rainbow Trout*	-	-		USGS 20916	?	11/8/2010	?	?	?
Rainbow Trout	450	-	Female	USGS 13283	3/30/2009	11/10/2010	590	60.2	402
Rainbow Trout	479	1225	Female	USGS 20911	?	11/19/2010	?	?	?
Brown Trout	551	1470	Male	3D9.1BF1CD4EDE	5/21/2005	11/29/2010	2018	87.4	230
Brown Trout	332	315	Female	3D9.1C2D8F0483	5/11/10	12/6/2010	205	79.03	309/ 294
Brown Trout	297	225	Female	3D9.1BF255F9ED	9/20/2007	12/11/2010	1178	82.5	229
Brown Trout	296	270	Female	3D9.1BF1D12101	?	12/16/2010	?	?	?
Brown Trout	480	890	Female	3D9.1C2D3D9D7D	?	12/18/2010	?	?	?
Rainbow Trout	295	240	Female	USGS 12706	5/8/2010	12/28/2010	?	30.5-30.6	268/ 203
Rainbow Trout	379	480	Female	USGS 20905	?	1/18/2011	?	?	?
Rainbow Trout	331	287.9	Male	USGS 20541	?	1/29/2011 e-fishing	?	? BAC RKM	?
Bluehead sucker	355	420	Female	3D9.1C2C469638	5/3/2007	2/1/11	?	1.45	335

*Found on shore on stringer near weir.

Electrofishing

The first electrofishing trip coincided with the installation of the weir. From October 27-29, 2010, 1,225 total fish were captured including 992 speckled dace (81.0%), 125 brown trout (10.2%), 104 rainbow trout (8.5%), and 4 bluehead suckers (<1%; Table 1). Some mortality of speckled dace occurred in October due to predation by trout in holding buckets during electrofishing passes; afterwards, small fish were held separately in buckets from larger fish. During a second electrofishing trip from January 25- February 3, 2011, a total of 1,975 fish were captured: 1,331 speckled dace (67.3%), 364 brown trout (18.4%), 243 rainbow trout (12.3%), and 37 bluehead sucker (2%; Table 1). See *Depletion Sampling* for more results.

Length frequency distributions for brown and rainbow trout (respectively) did not differ between the two sampling periods (Figure 12: BNT, Figure 13: RBT) However, more fish of each species were collected during the January electrofishing sample as it encompassed 2100 meters in contrast to the 600 meters covered during the October 2010 sample. Mean total length was similar for brown trout (Table 3) between samples, but significantly increased for rainbow trout from October to January electrofishing events ($p = 0.005$; Table 3). A subsample of speckled dace collected during each sample trip was measured. Based upon these measurements, speckled dace length frequency distributions (Figure 14) and mean total length did not differ between trips (Table 3). Only 4 bluehead sucker were collected during the October sample, making comparisons with the January sample problematic (Figure 15).

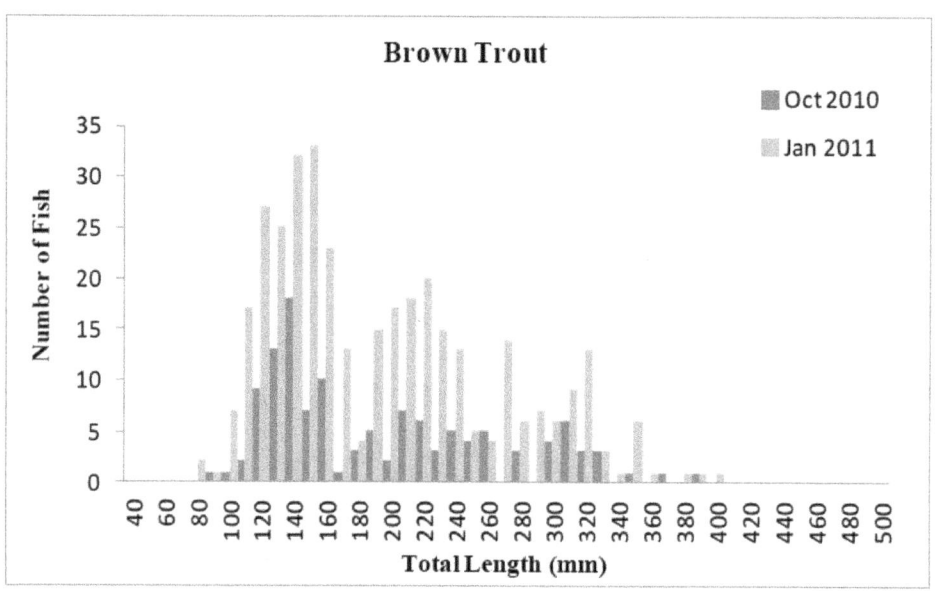

Figure 12. Length frequency histograms of brown trout collected in Bright Angel Creek during October 2010 and January 2011 electrofishing samples.

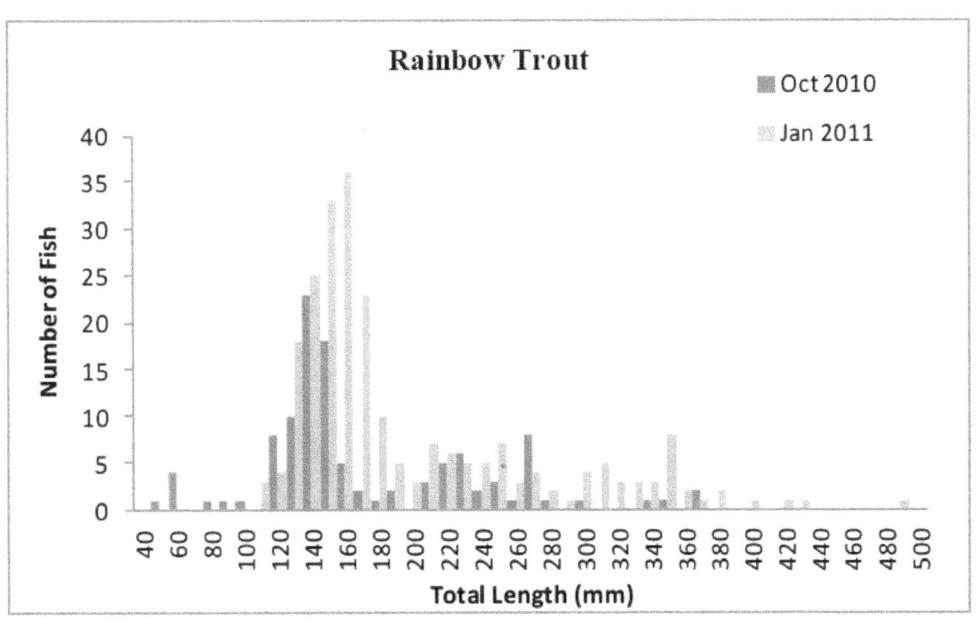

Figure 13. Length frequency histograms of rainbow trout collected in Bright Angel Creek during October 2010 and January 2011 electrofishing samples.

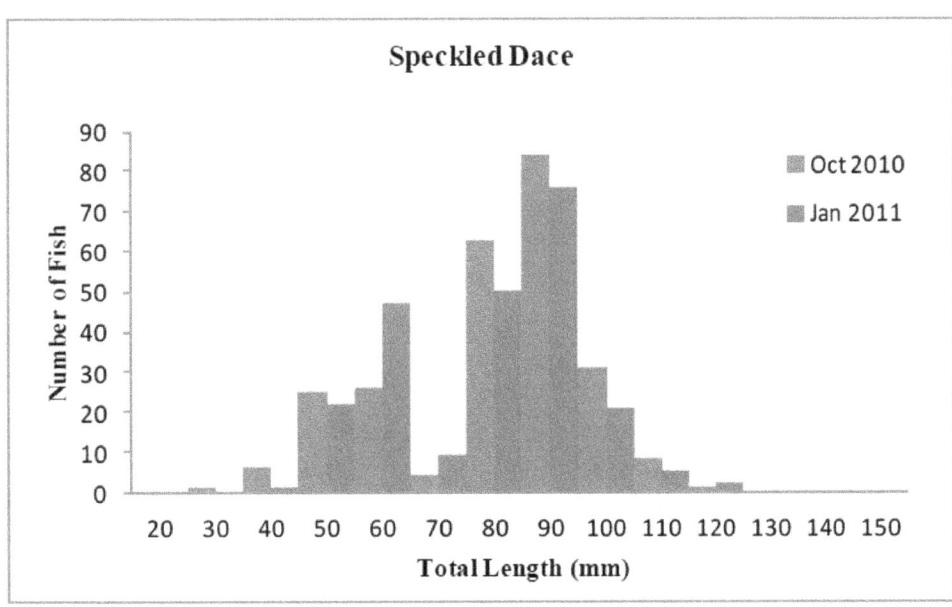

Figure 14. Length frequency histograms of speckled dace collected in Bright Angel Creek during October 2010 and January 2011 electrofishing samples. This figure represents the subsample of speckled dace collected were measured during each trip.

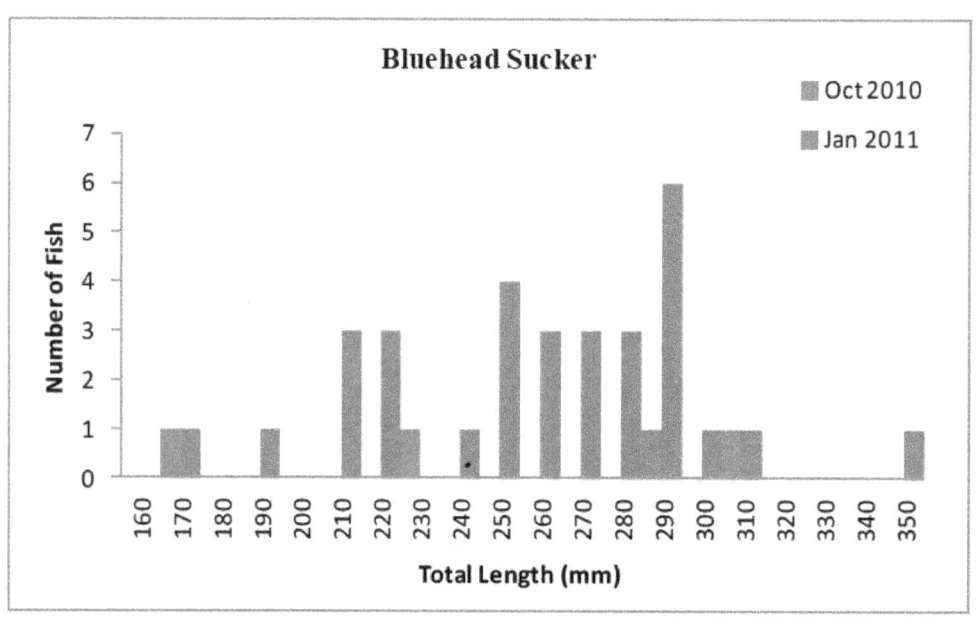

Figure 15. Length frequency histograms of bluehead sucker collected in Bright Angel Creek during October 2010 electrofishing and January 2011 electrofishing samples.

Table 3. Mean total length (TL), 95% confidence intervals, ranges, and *t*-test results for all species captured during electrofishing trips in October and January in Bright Angel Creek.

	October			January			
	Mean TL (mm)	95% CI	Range	Mean TL (mm)	95% CI	Range	*t*-test p values
Brown Trout	192.4	186.1-198.8	90-390	189.6	185.9-193.2	79-400	*p* = 0.69
Rainbow Trout	169.1	153.1-185.2	42-368	192.4	187.6-197.2	106-490	*p* = 0.005
Speckled Dace*	76.5	75.4-77.6	27-117	74.3	73.2-75.4	39-119	*p* = 0.15
Bluehead Sucker	258.4	252.1-264.7	179-355	251.8	219.3-284.2	170-312	*p* = 0.76

*Only a subset of speckled dace were measured.

Mean catch-per-unit-effort (CPUE) for the first pass of electrofishing was calculated for the creek sections that were sampled during both October and January trips (i.e. the first 600 meters). Mean CPUE significantly decreased for brown (p=0.009; Table 4) and rainbow trout (p=0.01; Table 4) and for speckled dace (p=0.04; Table 4) from the October to the January sampling trips. Bluehead sucker mean CPUE did not vary significantly (p=0.19; Table 4) from October to January trips (Table 4).

Table 4. Mean catch-per-unit-effort (CPUE), 95% confidence intervals, and *t*-test results from the lowest 600 meters of electrofishing sampling in October and January trips in Bright Angel Creek, by species.

| | October | | January | | |
	CPUE (fish/ 100 seconds)	95% CI	CPUE (fish/ 100 seconds)	95% CI	*t*-test p values
Brown Trout	0.68	0.60-0.76	0.34	0.26-0.43	*p* = 0.004
Rainbow Trout	0.56	0.47-0.65	0.26	0.19-0.32	*p* = 0.007
Speckled Dace	3.03	2.52-3.54	1.57	1.40-1.75	*p* = 0.02
Bluehead Sucker	0.02	0.007-0.033	0	-0.007-0.007	*p* = 0.09

Population Estimates

Analysis of electrofishing depletion data indicated that variation in trout capture probability was best explained by individual fish total length, while also accounting for behavioral responses to electrofishing across passes; therefore, the model containing these variables was used to derive parameters for abundance estimation. Average capture probability for trout declined after the first electrofishing pass from 0.45 to 0.31 using the most parsimonious model. Based on observed AIC weights, a secondary model incorporating trout behavioral response to electrofishing, total length, and season of sampling was ranked closely to the primary model, indicating potential differences in capture probability between October and January events (Table 5). Speckled dace capture probability varied widely between October and January sampling events (cumulative 3-pass capture efficiency of 0.40 vs. 0.12, respectively); therefore, season of sampling was included in the final model for speckled dace abundance estimation. Estimates of bluehead sucker using these methods were not attempted due to the relatively rare capture of the species in sampling reaches.

During 3-pass depletion sampling in October and January a high percentage of trout were removed (Table 5). For all stations sampled in October (6) and January (16), the cumulative proportion of the trout population removed was estimated to be between 54.8% and 88.6% (95% confidence interval) for rainbow and brown trout combined. Slightly higher depletions were achieved in October versus January (Table 5). Densities (number per 100 meters) of brown and rainbow trout in individual stations ranged from 8 – 50 and 6 – 44 individuals, respectively (Figure 16a, Figure 16b). Average brown trout density, including all stations, was similar in both January and October sampling events (24.8 and 28.0 trout/100-meters, *p* = 0.53; Figure 16a), but rainbow trout were 35% lower in abundance in January than October (17.4 and 26.9 trout/100-meters, *p* < 0.05; Figure 16b). Similar results were found in comparisons of only the lowest 600 meters of Bright Angel Creek where trout removal efforts were conducted during both seasons of sampling (Figure 17).

Table 5. Population estimates for all species except bluehead sucker from October 2010 and January 2011electrofishing trips in Bright Angel Creek. Bluehead sucker were not captured in sufficient number to generate population estimates.

	Oct. 26-30, 2010			Jan. 25-Feb. 3, 2011		
	Mean Pop. Estimate (No./100m)	95% CI	Capture/ Removal Efficiency (95% CI)	Mean Pop. Estimate (No./100m)	95% CI	Capture/ Removal Efficiency (95% CI)
Brown Trout	28	23-45	82% (63- 94)	25	20-41	70% (47-88)
Rainbow Trout	27	21-46	82% (63- 94)	17	14-30	70% (47-88)
Bluehead Sucker	--	--	--	--	--	--
Speckled Dace	411	305 -598	41% (29 – 55)	693	211 - 2947	11% (2 – 47)

As a result of low capture probability for speckled dace across both sampling events, abundance estimates lacked precision, particularly for January sites (Figure 18a, Figure 18b). Speckled dace density ranged from 155 to 1,788 per 100-meters including all sampling sites (Figure 18b). Total abundance of speckled dace in the lowest 600 meters, where trout removal was repeated in October and January, increased 55% from 2,465 (95% CI=1,831 – 3,587) to 5,482 (95% CI=1,669 - 23,263) individuals, however the change was not statistically significant ($p > 0.05$; Figure 18a, Figure 18b).

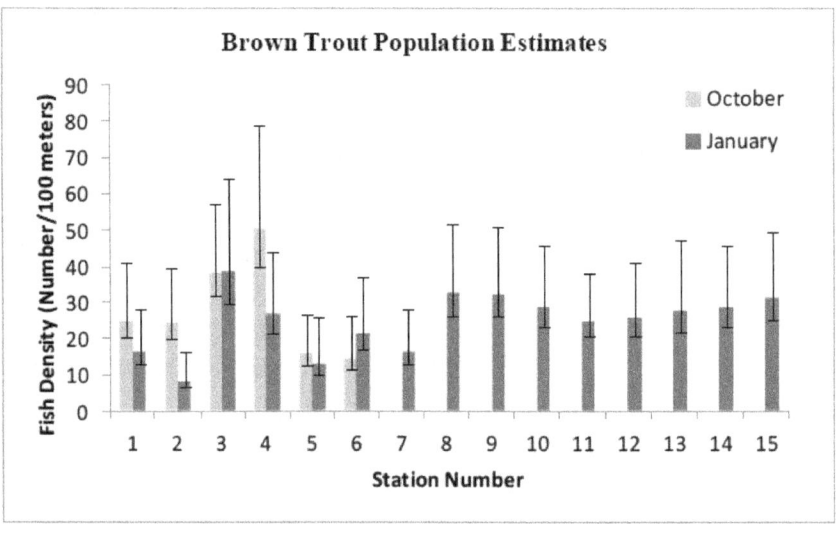

Figure 16a. Population estimates by electrofishing station in Bright Angel Creek for brown trout from electrofishing trips in October 2010 and January 2011 (with 95% confidence intervals).

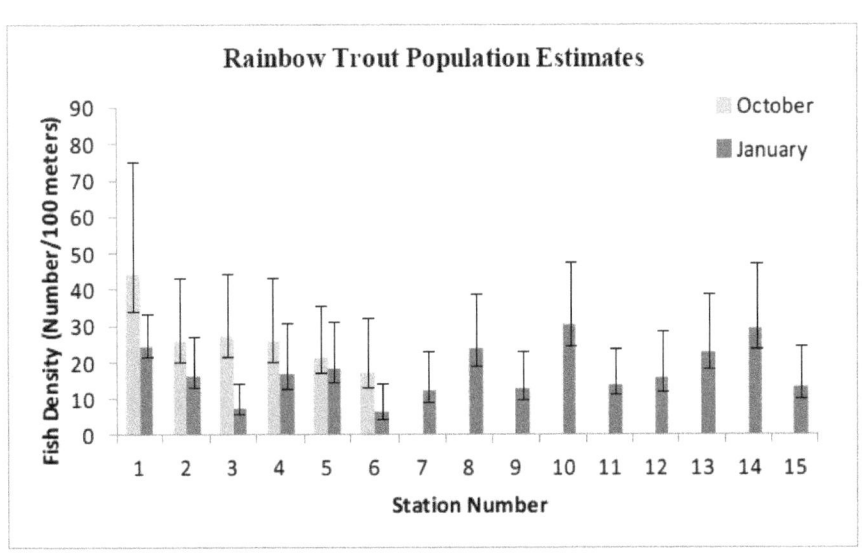

Figure 16b. Population estimates by electrofishing station in Bright Angel Creek for rainbow trout generated from electrofishing trips in October 2010 and January 2011 (with 95% confidence intervals).

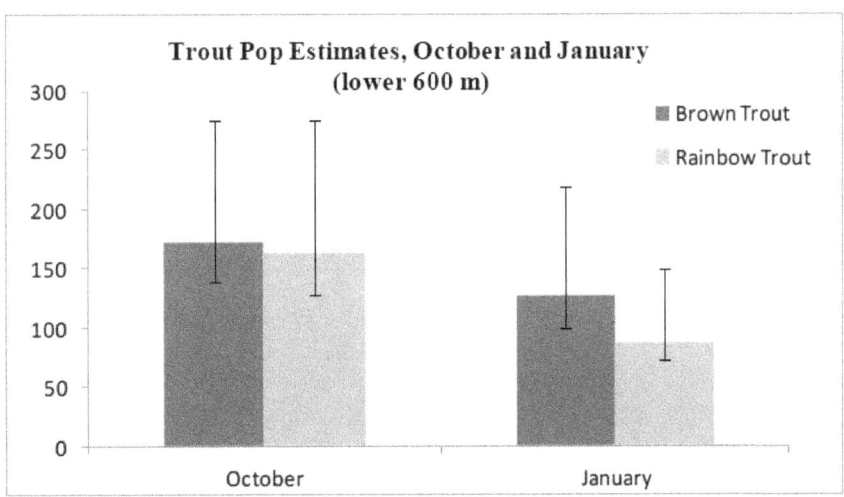

Figure 17. Population estimates for brown and rainbow trout for the lower 600 m of Bright Angel Creek generated from electrofishing trips in October 2010 and January 2011 (with 95% confidence intervals).

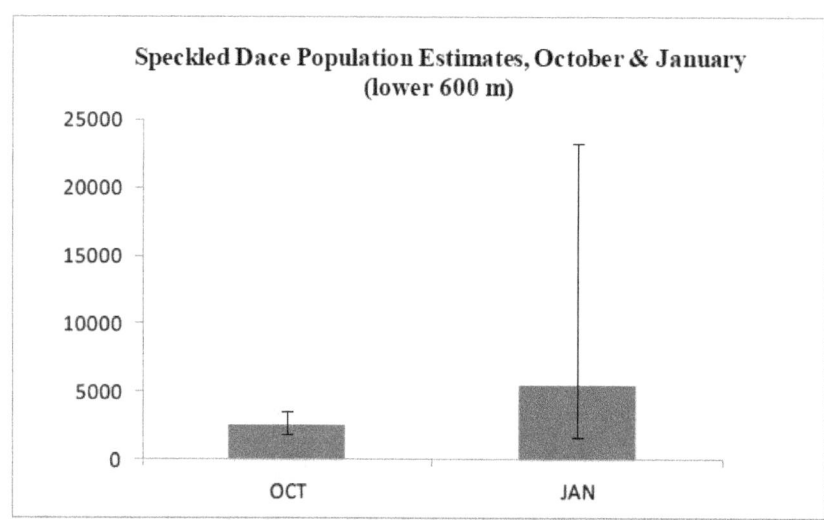

Figure 18a. Population estimates for speckled dace in Bright Angel Creek from electrofishing three pass depletion sampling in October 2010 and January 2011 combined.

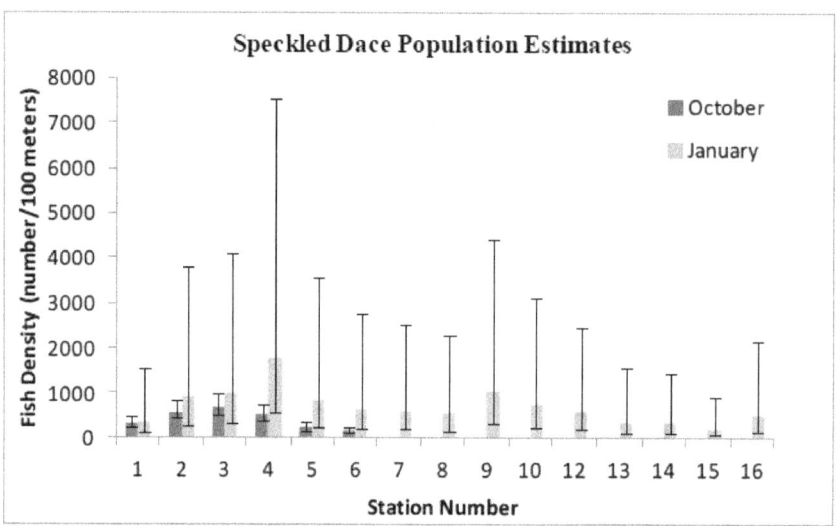

Figure 18b. Population estimates for speckled dace in Bright Angel Creek from electrofishing three pass depletion sampling in October 2010 and January 2011by electrofishing station.

Other Removal Methods

NPS anglers removed 26 rainbow trout and 9 brown trout from Bright Angel Creek during weir operations and during the January electrofishing effort (Table 1). No data were collected for angling efforts in the study area by private citizens.

Beneficial Use

Eighty-seven percent (946/1083) of the brown and rainbow trout captured and removed during the 2010-2011 Trout Reduction Project were consumed by the sampling crews (electrofishing and weir workers), NPS staff, Xanterra staff, and Phantom Ranch visitors. Of the 212 brown and rainbow trout caught using the weir, 211 were consumed. During the October 2010 electrofishing trip, 103 of the 229 brown and rainbow trout were consumed. All of the 607 brown and rainbow trout collected during the January 2011 electrofishing trip, as well as all 35 trout caught using angling gear were consumed.

Trophic and Diet Sampling

A total of 102 brown trout stomachs were collected and analyzed from the following size classes during each collection trip: 50-100 mm, 101-200 mm, 201-300 mm, and 301 mm and greater (Table 6). As many as 26 stomachs were analyzed from one size class from one trip, although in some cases samples were not available for each of size classes (Table 6).

Table 6. Numbers of stomachs by size class of brown and rainbow trout collected during October 2010 and January, June, and September sampling in Bright Angel Creek, Grand Canyon National Park.

Species	Time	50-100	101-200	201-300	> 300
Brown Trout	October 2010	0	3	1	0
	January 2011	2	16	7	6
	June 2011	3	18	7	19
	September 2011	5	11	3	1
	total	*10*	*48*	*18*	*26*
Rainbow Trout	October 2010	0	0	17	2
	January 2011	5	17	13	26
	June 2011	5	19	6	9
	September 2011	1	13	0	2
	total	*11*	*49*	*36*	*39*

Preliminary results from the stomach samples indicate that brown and rainbow trout feed on a variety of resources throughout the year, with aquatic insects being the primary prey type in all collections and annually (Table 6, Figure 19, Figure 20). Ephemeroptera (Baetidae), Diptera (Simuliidae, Chironomidae), Trichoptera (Hydropsychidae), and Megaloptera (Corydalidae) were the dominant groups of aquatic insects consumed by non-native trout in Bright Angel Creek. The mean proportion by weight (mg) of native fish in non-native stomachs varied between 2-33% for brown trout and 1-23% for rainbow trout throughout the year (Figure 19, Figure 20). Overall, piscivory rates (number of incidences of piscivory/ total number of stomachs examined) were 18% for brown trout and 5% for rainbow trout. Fish consumption was highest in October 2010 for brown trout and highest in September 2011 for rainbow trout (Figure 19, Figure 20). Speckled dace accounted for 95% of all fish consumed, with bluehead sucker the remaining 5%. Organic matter (primarily filamentous algae) consumption was higher in rainbow trout than in brown trout throughout the year, accounting for 10-51% of the diet by weight (Figure 19, Figure 20). Stable isotope analyses are currently in progress. Preliminary δ^{13}C and δ^{15}N values indicate non-native trout occupy the highest trophic level throughout the year in Bright Angel Creek.

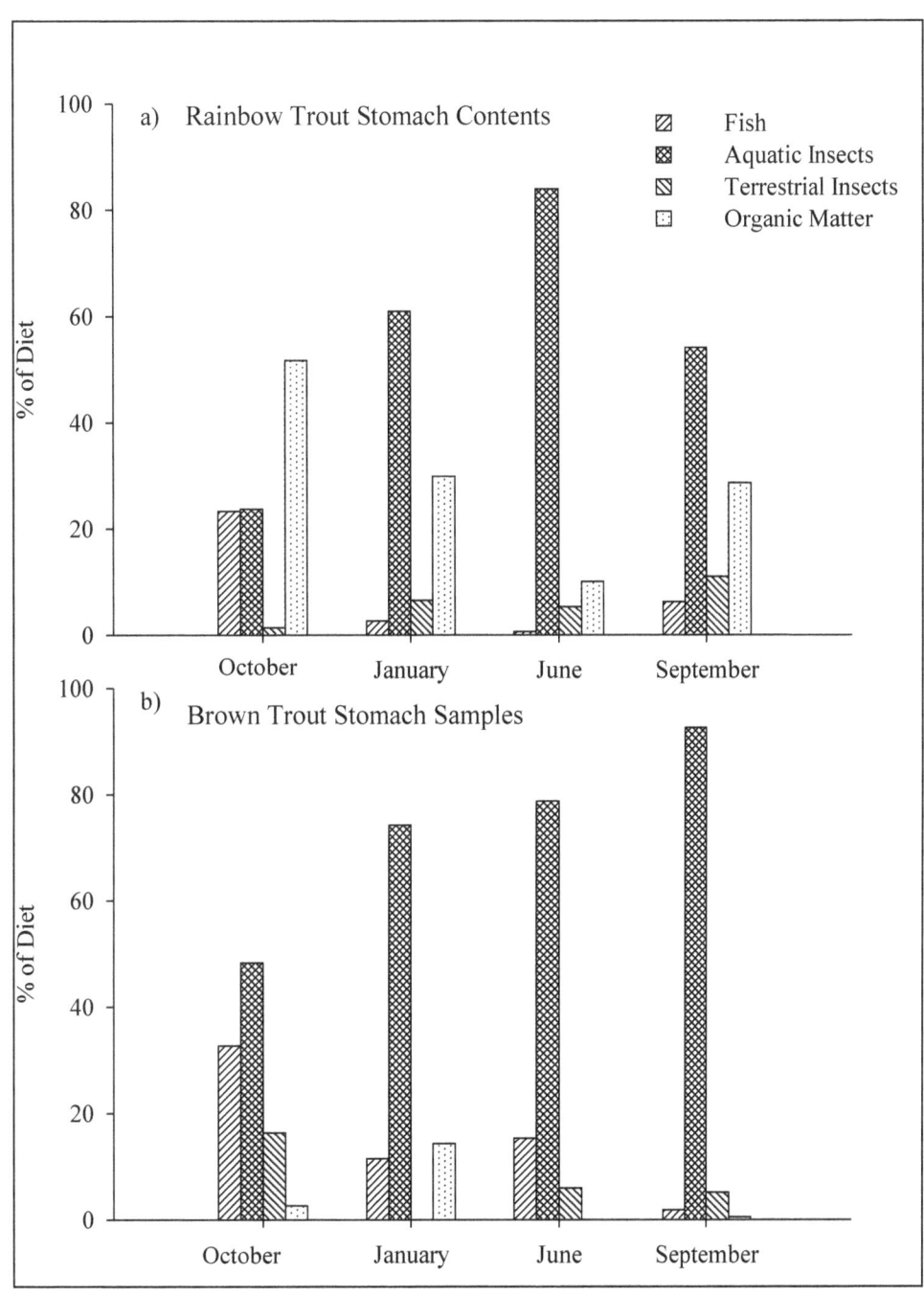

Figure 19. Mean proportions by weight (mg) of diet items present in stomachs sampled from Bright Angel Creek electrofishing samples for a) rainbow trout and b) brown trout.

29

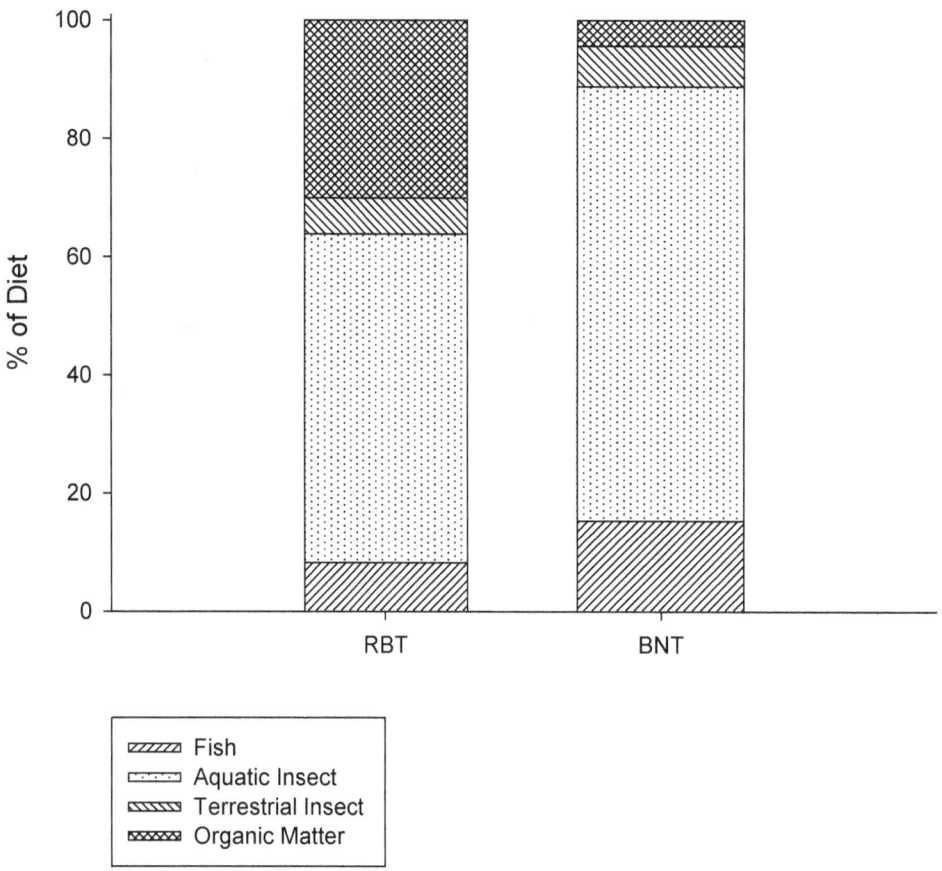

Figure 20. Total percentage of diet from rainbow and brown trout stomach samples collected in October 2010, and January, June and September 2011 from Bright Angel Creek.

Public Outreach

Between November 2, 2010 and February 4, 2011 project biologists made 116 visitor contacts. These contacts included individuals and groups of between 1 and 15 individuals in and around Bright Angel Creek and at Phantom Ranch, as well as on the South Kaibab trail. Contacts ranged from brief interactions of several minutes to lengthy hour-long discussions. Eighty-six contacts (74%) responded in a positive way to non-native control efforts. Nine contacts (8%) had a negative response to control efforts. The remaining contacts had neutral or undetermined opinions about control efforts. Self-identified anglers and angling groups accounted for 28 visitor contacts (24%), of which, 21 groups (75%) were angling during that trip.

Discussion

Weir

The weir was installed in Bright Angel Creek earlier in 2010-11 than in previous years of operation. Ripe females of both rainbow and brown trout were captured within 2 days of the initiation of the project, suggesting that at least part of the spawning run may have occurred prior to weir installation. The majority of brown and rainbow trout captured in the weir were in spawning condition. The timing of weir installation was based upon recommendations from Leibfried et al. (2005) and Sponholtz et al. (2010), and was aimed at spanning the spawning migrations of brown and rainbow trout from the Colorado River into Bright Angel Creek; however, the extent of movements of trout outside of late October through early February are unknown. Based on a review of the timing of brown trout captures during weir operations in 2006-07 (Sponholtz et al. 2010) and 2002-03 (Leibfried et al. 2005), as well as for 2010-11 (this report), it appears that run timing is variable and influenced by stream temperature (i.e. low night time temperatures result in fewer weir captures). Nevertheless, 84% of the observed brown trout migration occurred during 45 days in November and December in this study, suggesting that a majority of migrating brown trout were captured. A four day period in December accounted for 22% of rainbow trout migrations, but otherwise movements were less concentrated. Leibfried et al. (2005) and Sponholtz et al. (2010) suggested there may be a late January peak in rainbow trout spawning migration; however, no increase was observed during the 2010-11 weir installation. While little is known about the timing of rainbow trout spawning in Bright Angel Creek, Korman et al. (2011) found rainbow trout redd counts to peak between March and April in Glen Canyon. Korman also reported that spawning may occur as early as November and may extend into May (Dr. Josh Korman, Systems Ecologist, Ecometric Research Inc., email communication with Brian Healy, 12-11-11). Maddux and others found that in Nankoweap Creek in Grand Canyon National Park from 1984-1990, rainbow trout spawned from September through March (1987). In another study conducted in February-March 1990 in Nankoweap Creek, rainbow trout began migrating during the second week in February, with numbers peaking in early March (Leibfried and Montgomery 1993). From these results it appears that the timing of rainbow trout spawning migrations may be less concentrated in the fall than for brown trout, and movement of both species in other times of the year deserves more study.

Native and non-native fish tagging efforts by Arizona Game and Fish Department, U.S. Fish and Wildlife Service, University of Florida researchers (Near Shore Ecology study), and GCMRC have been underway for several years in Grand Canyon and these efforts are currently expanding (Ecometric Research, Inc.- Rainbow Trout Natal Origin study). GCMRC is working to update the centralized Grand Canyon fish database (William Persons, Fishery Biologist, Grand Canyon Monitoring and Research Center, email communication with Brian Healy, 11-14-11). Updated information on tagged fish, including the location and date of initial tagging, movement history, growth, etc. could inform not only this study, but many others in Grand Canyon. For instance, an unripe female rainbow trout removed using the weir in 2010-11 was initially tagged near the Little Colorado River, critical habitat and primary spawning ground for endangered humpback chub in Grand Canyon. A second was tagged near another potentially important aggregation of humpback chub in the Colorado River, 30 mile, in which evidence of spawning has been posited (Valdez and Masslich 1999, Anderson et al. 2010). These mainstem fish were utilizing Bright Angel Creek, perhaps to spawn, suggesting that reproduction and movement in rainbow trout may be more widespread than previously known. All of the tagged brown trout captured in the weir that were locatable in the GCMRC database had been initially tagged in the Colorado River within 10 miles of Bright Angel Creek. However, in previous years, brown trout that had been tagged as far away as 34 miles upstream (RM 53.9; Leibfried et al. 2005) and 89 miles downstream (RM 176.4; Sponholtz et al. 2010) were captured in the weir. Efforts will continue to locate and interpret the missing records as the GCMRC fish database is updated.

Electrofishing and Depletion Sampling

Capture probability differed for both trout and speckled dace between October and January electrofishing trips. This information can be used to refine sampling methods. Factors that could affect capture probability include crew experience, reduced visibility due to glare, electrofishing settings, water temperature, habitat complexity, fish behavior, net mesh size, net damage, and fish size. Although 82% depletions were achieved for both brown and rainbow trout in the lower 600 meters of Bright Angel Creek during the October electrofishing trip, only rainbow trout exhibited a decrease in density there; brown trout density remained unchanged. Because the weir was in place almost continuously during this time period blocking entry from the Colorado River, and size structure of brown trout did not differ between electrofishing sampling events, this return of brown trout to the electrofishing reach indicates that fish are likely immigrating from upstream reaches of Bright Angel Creek. While the weir was not in operation for 8 days in December, it is unlikely that the lower 600 meters was repopulated by brown trout from the Colorado River during that time as no fish were captured as flow and turbidity increased in the days prior to the removal of the weir. Because fish smaller than approximately 200 millimeters total length are assumed to pass through the mesh of the weir, a decrease in average size or shift in size structure toward smaller individuals might be expected if recolonization occurred from reaches downstream of the weir or the Colorado River. There were no differences in mean fish total length or length frequency for brown trout and speckled dace between trips; however, rainbow trout increased in total length from October to January. Although measures were taken to account for common biases in depletion sampling, it is possible that the capture efficiency estimates are incorrect, resulting in more fish remaining in the creek after the October electrofishing sample. Further study during subsequent years of electrofishing and weir operations will reveal whether this trend continues.

Trophic and Diet Sampling

Analyses of both stomach and trophic samples are ongoing by University of Missouri researchers. Preliminary results indicate that non-native trout in Bright Angel Creek are piscivorous, consuming varied amounts of native fish throughout the year, as well as other resources. As in the mainstem Colorado River (Yard et al. 2011), non-native trout preferentially consume native versus non-native fish (e. g., other trout) in Bright Angel Creek. Only native fish were found in trout stomachs. Trout also seem to inhabit the highest trophic level throughout the creek. Final results will provide insight into native fish restoration efforts, including for humpback chub, in Bright Angel Creek.

Recommendations

- Continue with weir operation to intercept brown and rainbow trout entering Bright Angel Creek from the Colorado River. Install the weir earlier to more completely cover the brown trout spawning period to provide additional insight into spawning migrations and improve weir efficiency. Weir placement beneath the lower bridge resulted in interference with GCMRC hydrology equipment (Dr. David Topping, Research Hydrologist, Grand Canyon Monitoring and Research Center, personal communication with Brian Healy). Consider placing the weir in a different location for future installations.

- The weir is targeted for the capture of mature, spawning fish. Although trout as small as 135 millimeters total length have been captured in the weir (this report), it appears that the weir is most effective in capturing fish greater than or equal to 200 millimeters total length. If smaller fish are to be targeted, the weir should be redesigned with smaller mesh, and/or made to be bi-directional.

- Electrofishing efforts may need to be expanded upstream to offset apparently high immigration rates if low abundance of trout is to be maintained in the long-term to benefit native fish.

- Continue to investigate methods to improve capture efficiency during depletion sampling.

- Continue to search the GCMRC centralized fish database for records of tagged fish captured during Bright Angel Creek weir and electrofishing operations.

- Continue and expand public outreach efforts. Update Grand Canyon National Park website to include information about the Bright Angel Creek Trout Reduction project and produce a site bulletin to reach more visitors as well as NPS and Xanterra employees.

Literature Cited

Anderson, M.E., M.W. Ackerman, K.D. Hilwig, A.E. Fuller, and P.D. Alley. 2010. Evidence of young humpback chub overwintering in the mainstem Colorado River, Marble Canyon, Arizona, USA. The Open Fish Science Journal 3: 42-50.

Carothers, S. W. and C. O. Minckley. 1981. A survey of the fishes, aquatic invertebrates and aquatic plants of the Colorado River and selected tributaries from Lee Ferry to Separation Rapids. Final Report to Water and Power Resources Service, Contract No. 7-07-30-X0026. Museum of Northern Arizona, Flagstaff, AZ.

Coggins, Jr., L.G., M.D. Yard, and W.E. Pine III. 2011. Nonnative fish control in the Colorado River in Grand Canyon, Arizona: An effective program or serendipitous timing? Transactions of the American Fisheries Society: 140:456:470.

Cooch E., and G. White. 2011. Program MARK: a gentle introduction. 9th Addition. Colorado State University. Ft. Collins, Colorado.

Dexter National Fish Hatchery and Technology Center. 2010. A genetic management plan for captive and translocated endangered humpback chub in the lower Colorado River Basin. Final report, November 10.

Douglas, M.R., and M.E. Douglas. 2007. Genetic structure of humpback chub *Gila cypha* and roundtail chub *G. robusta* in the Colorado River ecosystem. Final report, Department of Fish, Wildlife and Conservation Biology, Colorado State University, Fort Collins, Colorado.

Gloss, S.P. and L.G. Coggins, 2005. Fishes of Grand Canyon in Gloss, S.P., Lovich, J.E., and Melis, T.S., eds., The state of the Colorado River ecosystem in Grand Canyon: USGS Circular 1282, pp. 33-56.

Grand Canyon Wildlands Council and SWCA, Inc. 2006. Humpback chub translocation in Grand Canyon: Feasibility and experimental design. Unpublished report submitted to Grand Canyon National Park, April 1.

Grand Canyon Wildlands Council. 2010. Humpback chub translocation into Shinumo Creek, Grand Canyon National Park. Unpublished final report submitted to Grand Canyon National Park, August 25.

Healy, B.D., E. Omana Smith, J.J. Spurgeon, C. Paukert, J. Whittier, P.J. Sponholtz, B. Leibfried. 2011a. Translocation of humpback chub to Grand Canyon tributaries and related nonnative fish control activities: 2010 Annual Report. Unpublished report submitted to Bureau of Reclamation, Interagency Agreement Number: 09-AA-40-2890, May 4.

Healy, B.D., E. Omana Smith, L. Belica. 2011b. Shinumo Creek humpback chub monitoring and translocation #3, June 12-25, 2011, Trip Report. Unpublished report submitted to the Upper Colorado Region, Bureau of Reclamation, Interagency Agreement Number: 09-AA-40-2890, August 4.

Huntoon, P.W. 1970. The hydro-mechanics of the groundwater system in the southern portion of the Kaibab Plateau, Arizona. Ph.D. Dissertation, University of Arizona, Tucson, Arizona.

Korman, J., M. Kaplinski, T. S. Melis. 2011. Effects of fluctuating flows and a controlled flood on incubation success and early survival rates and growth of age-0 rainbow trout in a large regulated river. Transactions of the American Fisheries Society 140(2): 487-505.

Leibfried, W.L and W.L. Montgomery. 1993. Regulated flows, trout spawning, and abundance of bald eagles on the Colorado River, Grand Canyon National Park. *In:* Proceeding of the First Biennial Conference on Research in Colorado Plateau National Parks, Rowlands, van Riper, and Sogge eds. Northern Arizona University, Flagstaff, Arizona July 22-25, 1991.

Leibfried, W., L. Johnstone, S. Rhodes, and M. Lauretta. 2005. Feasibility Study to determine the efficacy of using a weir in Bright Angel Creek to capture brown trout. Unpublished final report submitted to Grand Canyon National Park, SWCA Project # 6462-091, November 10.

Maddux, H.R., D.M. Kubly, J.C. deVos, Jr., W.R. Persons, R. Staedicke, and R.L. Wright. 1987. Effects of varied flow regimes on aquatic resources of Glen and Grand canyons. Glen Canyon Environmental Studies Final Report, U.S. Bureau of Reclamation, Upper Colorado Region, Salt Lake City, Utah. 291 pp.

Makinster, A.S., Persons, W.R., Avery, L.A., and Bunch, A.J., 2010, Colorado River fish monitoring in Grand Canyon, Arizona; 2000 to 2009 summary: U.S. Geological Survey Open-File Report 2010-1246, 26 p.

Minckley, C.O. 1978. A report on aquatic investigation conducted during 1976-1977, on Bright Angel, Phantom, and Pipe Creeks, Grand Canyon National Park, Coconino County, Arizona. Annual investigators report submitted to Grand Canyon National Park. Department of BiologicalSciences, Northern Arizona University, and Biology Department, Museum of Northern Arizona, Flagstaff.

National Park Service. 2006. Finding of no significant impact: Bright Angel Creek trout reduction project, Grand Canyon National Park.

National Park Service. 2006. NPS Management Policies. U. S. Dept. of Interior, Washington, D. C. 168 pages.

National Park Service. 1995. Grand Canyon National Park's General Management Plan. Grand Canyon, Arizona.

Otis IV, E.O. 1994. Distribution, abundance, and composition of fishes in Bright Angel and Kanab creeks, Grand Canyon National Park, Arizona. Thesis, University of Arizona, Tucson, Arizona.

Peterson, J. T., R. F. Thurow, and J. W. Guzevich. 2004. An evaluation of multi-pass electrofishing for estimating the abundance of stream dwelling salmonids. Transactions of the American Fisheries Society 133:462-475.

Saunders, W. C., K. D. Fausch, G. C. White. 2011. Accurate estimation of salmonid abundance in small streams using nighttime removal electrofishing: an evaluation using marked fish. Transactions of the American Fisheries Society 31(2): 403-415.

Speas, D.W. 2002. Annual Report. Arizona Game and Fish Department. Unpublished report prepared for the Grand Canyon Monitoring and Research Center, Flagstaff, AZ.

Sponholtz, P.J., P. B. Holton, D.R. VanHaverbeke. 2010. Bright Angel Creek Trout Reduction Project Summary Report on 2006-2007 weir and electrofishing efforts. Unpublished draft report updated and resubmitted to Grand Canyon National Park, December.

Sponholtz, P.J., E. Omana Smith, B. Healy. 2011. Havasu Creek native fish monitoring, October 7-13, 2011 Trip Report. Unpublished report prepared for the Upper Colorado River Region, Bureau of Reclamation, Interagency Agreement Number: 09-AA-2890. November 10.

U.S. Fish and Wildlife Service. 2008. Final biological opinion on the operation of Glen Canyon Dam. U.S. Fish and Wildlife Service, Phoenix, Arizona.

Usher, H.D., W.C. Leibfried, D.W. Blinn, and S. W. Carothers. 1984. A survey of present and future impacts of water depletions and additions o the aquatic and terrestrial habitats of Roaring Springs, Bright Angel, Garden, and Pipe Creeks, Grand Canyon National Park. Final Report to U.S. Department of the Interior, CX 8000-9-0032. San Francisco, California.

Valdez, R.A. and R.J. Ryel. 1995. Life history and ecology of the humpback chub (*Gila cypha*) in the Colorado River, Grand Canyon, Arizona. Report # TR-250-08. BIO/WEST, Inc., Logan, Utah.

Valdez, R.A. and W.J. Masslich. 1999. Evidence of reproduction by humpback chub in a warm spring of the Colorado River in Grand Canyon, Arizona. The Southwestern Naturalist 44: 384-387.

Valdez, R.A., S.W. Carothers, M.E. Douglas, M. Douglas, R.J. Ryel, K.R. Bestgen, and D.L. Wegner. 2000. Research and implementation plan for establishing a second population of humpback chub in Grand Canyon, Final Report to U.S. Department of the Interior, U.S. Geological Survey, Grand Canyon Monitoring and Re-search Center, Flagstaff, Arizona.

Voichick, N., and S.A. Wright. 2007. Water-temperature data for the Colorado River and tributaries between Glen Canyon Dam and Spencer Canyon, northern Arizona, 1988–2005: U.S. Geological Survey Data Series 251, 24 p.

White, G. C. 2008. Closed population estimation models and their extensions in Program MARK. Environmental and Ecological Statistics 15:89-99.

White, G. C., and K. P. Burnham. 1999. Program MARK: survival estimation from populations of marked animals. Bird Study 46, supplement 120-139.

Yard, M.D., L.G. Coggins, C.V. Baxter, G.E. Bennett, and J. Korman. 2011. Trout piscivory in the Colorado River, Grand Canyon: Effects of turbidity, temperature, and fish prey availability. Transactions of the American Fisheries Society: 140:471:486.

Appendix A: Trip participants, affiliations, and roles during 2010-2011 Bright Angel Creek season.

Bright Angel Creek Weir, October 25, 2010 – February 4, 2011		
Name	Affiliation	Role
Dan Whiting	UM	Senior Research Assistant
Emily Omana	NPS	GRCA Fisheries Biologist
Brian Healy	NPS	GRCA Fisheries Program Manager
Jeremy White	NPS	GRCA Wildlife Biologist
Pam Sponholtz	USFWS-Flagstaff	Fisheries Biologist
Nathan Chase	USFWS-Flagstaff	Fisheries Intern
Martha Hahn	NPS	GRCA Chief, Science and Resource Management
Marianne Crawford	BOR	
Betsy Herrmann	GRCA	Volunteer
Bryan Smith	GRCA	Volunteer
Susie Healy	GRCA	Volunteer
Sarah Mueting	GRCA	Volunteer
Bright Angel Creek Electrofishing, October 25-30, 2010		
Name	Affiliation	Role
Brian Healy	NPS- Crew Lead	GRCA Fisheries Program Manager
Emily Omana	NPS	GRCA Fisheries Biologist
Dan Whiting	UM	Senior Research Assistant
Mitch Thorson	USFWS-Parker	Fisheries Biologist

Tammy Knecht	USFWS-Parker	Research Technician
Olajawon Pusher	USFWS-Pinetop	Technician
Ryan Slattery	USFWS-Pinetop	Technician

Bright Angel Creek Electrofishing, January 24 – 30, 2011		
Name	Affiliation	Role
Emily Omana	NPS- Crew Lead	GRCA Fisheries Biologist
Dan Whiting	University of Missouri	Senior Research Assistant
Jon Spurgeon	University of Missouri	Graduate Student
Sam Gordon	Grand Canyon Trust	Volunteer
Dan Shein	Grand Canyon Trust	Volunteer
Denise Hudson	Grand Canyon Trust	Volunteer
Bill Kluwin	Grand Canyon Trust	Volunteer
Gisela Kluwin	Grand Canyon Trust	Volunteer

Bright Angel Creek Electrofishing, January 29, 2011 – February 5, 2011		
Name	Affiliation	Role
Brian Healy	NPS – Crew Lead	GRCA Fisheries Program Manager
Dan Whiting	University of Missouri	Senior Research Assistant
Dave Speas	Bureau of Reclamation	Fisheries Biologist
Melissa Trammell	NPS – IMR	Fisheries Biologist
Dan Shein	Grand Canyon Trust	Volunteer
Dean Wadsworth	Grand Canyon Trust	Volunteer
Kathy Hilton	Grand Canyon Trust	Volunteer
Bill Ahearn	Grand Canyon Trust	Volunteer
Susan Ahearn	Grand Canyon Trust	Volunteer

Appendix B: Bright Angel Creek Trout Reduction Project informational poster displayed at Phantom Ranch.

Grand Canyon National Park

National Park Service
U.S. Department of the Interior

Native Fish Conservation at Phantom Ranch

Something Weir is Going On

Just downstream of the lower Bright Angel Creek bridge, the National Park Service in partnership with the Bureau of Reclamation and the U.S. Fish and Wildlife Service installed a weir (fish trap) to catch spawning brown trout and rainbow trout in Bright Angel Creek.

The weir in Bright Angel Creek will be operated and trout will be removed from the creek throughout the brown trout spawning season (October - February).

Removing Non-native Fish from Bright Angel Creek

This project is being conducted to help offset human-caused changes to the aquatic habitat in the Colorado River basin. A long-term decline in native and an increase in non-native fish populations in Grand Canyon National Park have caused concern among fisheries managers.

The dual purposes of this project are to benefit humpback chub and other native fish in the Colorado River, and to enhance the native fish community that once flourished in Bright Angel Creek. Trout from Bright Angel Creek travel long distances and prey on native fish found in other parts of the river system, such as the Little Colorado River. Also, non-native fish outcompete native fish for food and habitat.

Bright Angel Creek historically supported an assemblage of native fish that adapted to the dynamic conditions of the natural Colorado River and its tributaries. Two men with a string of humpback chub. Colorado River near Phantom Ranch Circa 1919.

Restoring Balance to Critical Habitat

Today, trout dominate the fish assemblage in Bright Angel Creek. By removing migrating brown trout and interrupting the annual spawning cycle, the endangered humpback chub and other native fish will benefit through reduced numbers of non-native fish and thereby decreased losses due to predation.

For more information contact:
Brian Healy (928) 638-7453
Emily Omana (928) 638-7477

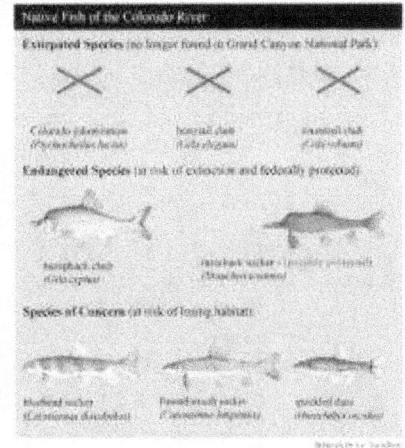

Native Fish of the Colorado River

Extirpated Species (no longer found in Grand Canyon National Park)

Colorado pikeminnow
(Ptychocheilus lucius)

bonytail chub
(Gila elegans)

roundtail chub
(Gila robusta)

Endangered Species (at risk of extinction and federally protected)

humpback chub
(Gila cypha)

razorback sucker (possibly extirpated)
(Xyrauchen texanus)

Species of Concern (at risk of losing habitat)

bluehead sucker
(Catostomus discobolus)

flannelmouth sucker
(Catostomus latipinnis)

speckled dace
(Rhinichthys osculus)

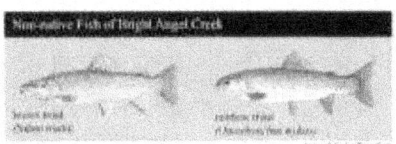

Non-native Fish of Bright Angel Creek

brown trout
(Salmo trutta)

rainbow trout
(Oncorhynchus mykiss)

41

NPS 113/118207, December 2012